Side by Side

Tales from Behind the Canvas

KIM YESIS

Side by Side Tales from Behind the Canvas

"Most of us go to our graves with our music still inside us."
—Oliver Wendell Holmes.

I didn't want that for Peter.

Other books by Kim Yesis:

The Mayenne Bay Series Novels:

Artifice

Brush with Fire - coming soon

Artist in the Allagash, *a wilderness journal*

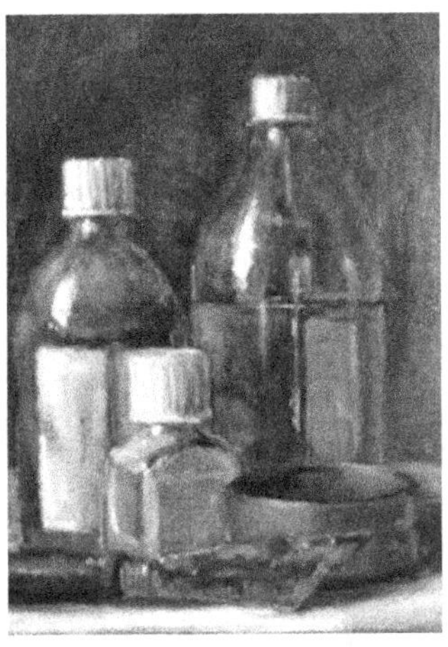

1

The Background Makes the Painting

"Go the distance."
—Field of Dreams

Planted on the Nova Scotia sand, intentionally disconnected from computer and phone without a single human in view, we could talk openly and without distraction. Yet, we weren't talking openly. We were barely talking at all.

"I can't get work out of my head," I grumbled, looking over at Peter's brooding face. He returned no answer. My stomach tightened. Why had we come all this way if he wasn't even going to speak? "If this place can't inspire us..." I tried again, leaving the thought dangling for him to complete. Again, no response, though I could see his jaw furiously working the tension. I breathed an exhausted sigh. Each attempt at conversation this morning had fizzled into silence and furrowed brows and, once again, we both turned our eyes vaguely to the sea.

Abruptly, Peter swung around, kicking his coffee cup in the same motion, and with a penetrating look, blurted, "What I *really* want is to be an *artist!*" The words tripped clumsily from his mouth as if they'd been stuck in his throat for ages and had finally broken free.

I stared up at him.

"What did you say?" I asked without needing to as I mechanically blotted the mess with my napkin.

"I want to be an artist, a painter." he spoke more softly, searching my face for a reaction.

An artist, I repeated to myself. To my own surprise, I didn't choke on my coffee. Instead, I slowly turned this declaration over in my mind like I was tasting a new food for the first time. I had urged Peter to pursue art since the early days of our marriage when he'd shown so much promise coming out of school. He had declined, lacking confidence, and instead had made a 25-year detour into engineering. How often had I joked that he was actually an artist masquerading as an engineer? The daring he lacked as a young man was evident in his eyes now as he waited for my answer.

It was the first time either of us had heard his wish spoken aloud and probably the first time Peter had consciously realized it. He was the first to break the stunned silence.

"OK, that surprised even me," he admitted, laughing and plopping down on the blanket beside me.

What a momentous change to consider 2000 miles from home. We had been to Nova Scotia before, but the secluded spot we'd discovered off the northern end of the Marine Drive far surpassed our previous destinations in isolation and utter noiselessness. Sequestered beside the ocean in a quiet this limitless, it was the daily grind that felt alien, surreal.

I refilled Peter's cup, and between sips of scalding coffee, words began to flow as we reviewed our situation. Son and daughter halfway through college. In-home care of an aging parent. Age 50 looming on the horizon. But these matters, we took in stride. Work was where the problem lay. I commuted an hour to a draining job while Peter traveled and toiled excessively at his. As we concluded the litany of our obligations on this last note, the stuck feeling in the pits of our stomachs intensified to an uncomfortable but familiar queasiness.

"I'll do anything to break free," I had promised Peter and the universe back home as we'd booked this trip.

"Me, too," he had echoed.

So, we had packed up and put as much distance as tuition bills would allow between ourselves and our misery just to mull over our future.

I mentally stepped back to consider our relationship in the face of his astonishing proposal. Our bond had begun in storybook fashion on the fortuitous day our grandmothers had given birth to our mothers in the same hospital room. Our mothers had afterward become girlhood friends, and this friendship had continued after marriage and children. Here sat Peter and I, the third generation of this extraordinary connection and a close couple since high school. This is the history that gave rise to two late forty-somethings sitting in the cool sea air of a deserted Nova Scotia beach unexpectedly contemplating a path to an art career.

Moments of critical change have always been the high energy points of Peter's and my relationship, and I instinctively knew we were on the brink of one of them. Suddenly, we were smiling at one another, every pore alive to his idea. *But, how would this work?* Peter read my thought, hopped up and began talking rapidly as if he'd been planning this for years.

"I wouldn't quit my job just yet. I have to see if I even have the talent for this."

Nodding my agreement, tears began rolling down my face, tears of—well, I don't know what. Happiness that Peter might finally become an artist? Joy that a change might be in the offing? Relief that an idea, any idea, had been born of this long journey? Certainly, there was no release from bondage for me in this scenario. I would continue work at one office or another. And yet, I felt strangely liberated and even excited. Any positive alteration was, at this point, welcome, and the idea of living alongside an artist had always held great appeal.

He stopped and added, "I would never quit unless you were in a job you liked."

Now the tears were really flowing.

I fished for a pen and paper from my sack and started mapping out a five-year plan. It's not that we had much information to go on or that five is particularly magical as a number. It's just that five years are enough to lift you over the present knot of problems, giving you a sense of release. They leave enough time to effect real change without fearing permanence if the plan turns out badly. Peter and I had made numerous five-year plans over the years. We'd learned from experience to include elements of flexibility and paths of escape. What is the good of unsticking yourself today if you will only feel stuck again tomorrow?

These plans are most at risk at the very beginning, when the pull of the old life is still high, and you're teeter-tottering between the present and the future.

"We need some kind of action to jump start the process," I asserted without a clue what that was. I was astonished to find that Peter had the answer ready.

"I think I need to find a local artists' group and a way to exhibit a painting or two into an area competition to get some feedback."

Yes. A reality orientation test. Put down some paint and see what happens. Suddenly, the queasiness was gone, and the air between us was crackling with current. Call it midlife crisis, call it desperation. I called it inspiration, and it was exhilarating.

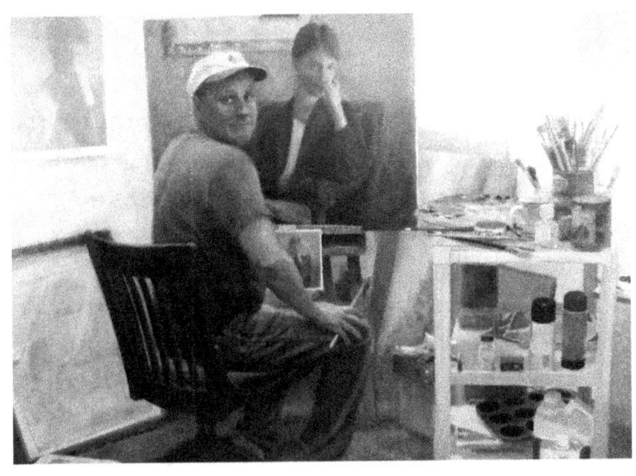

2

First Brush

"The future is always beginning now."
—Mark Strand

On the plane ride home, my mind whirled with ideas.

"Do you think five years is enough for the first, let's call it the *fitness* stage?" I asked Peter. "You haven't picked up a brush for years." I saw in my mind's eye the easel he'd rarely put to use but dragged from house to house every time we'd moved. "It'll be a slower process having to maintain a full-time job while you're rekindling skills."

"If I'm still unsure after five years, I'll have my answer," he assured me.

We arrived home from Nova Scotia elated but acutely aware that Peter's endeavor would be an uphill climb. Minutes after stepping over our living room threshold, Nova Scotia sand still in his shoes, Peter was pacing off the basement for his studio. This was a positive sign and a necessary exercise, but every artist (and every artist's sidekick) knows the difference between setting up a studio so you *feel* like an artist and producing paintings so that you *are* one. He had a lot of work to do.

Outfitting the studio was an adventure unto itself. We wandered through every aisle of the art supply store for the better part of a morning.

"I love the smells. It's like buying new school supplies," I said giddily, inhaling the fresh paper fumes and caressing the journals as we passed the water color and sketch pad stock. Peter, who did not share my love of the classroom, rolled his eyes and began tossing things into the basket. "You hate oils," I reminded him, as tube after tube of oil paint landed in the cart. "You've told me over and over again that you weren't good at them in school. Besides, your water colors and pastels are fabulous. Why make this harder than it has to be?"

"I want to work at something more lasting," he explained, characteristically distilling hours of reflection into a single sentence that exploded in my mind. This whole idea had obviously been percolating in the back of his head for a long time. Looking back, I should have just been grateful that he'd already narrowed his media down to one.

Watching the number on the cash register rise, it was clear this was going to take more than just courage.

"How do budding artists afford this stuff?" I asked him.

"They have a side job," he shrugged simply, then added with a sly grin, "or a very supportive partner."

"Flatterer," I threw back at him.

Inwardly, I was warmed by his recognition and gratified by my contribution. Even as the fitness plan kicked into gear, I was conscious that, while it was Peter's talent that would drive his career (or not), this would be a shared endeavor, a side-by-side enterprise. At this early stage, I had no idea what this actually meant but I plunged ahead anyway like a swimmer who accepts that the first dip may be bracingly cold. It took a series of trips to the art supply store to fully equip the studio. Somehow, a new easel made its way into the car to replace the perfectly good studio easel we'd hauled around for years, but I couldn't begrudge Peter this singular indulgence.

Predictably, setting up the studio had been the easy part. About a week later, I dropped down into the cellar to find him sitting completely still in his chair, shoulders sagging, clean brush in hand, staring at an empty canvas. Old soup and tomato sauce cans filled with untouched paint brushes and tools cluttered his workspace. Strewn all around him on the floor were art books about Homer, van Gogh, Wyeth, Whistler, and Eakins along with old issues of *Southwest Art* and *American Art Review*. He held open on his lap books on Rockwell and Rembrandt, two of his favorite artists.

"Something wrong?" I asked the obvious.

He started bewilderedly as if roused from sleep.

"Can't decide what to paint," he said, emerging from his daze. "I've always liked landscapes, but we're in Iowa. Great Plains landscapes —the farmlands here, anyway—really don't excite me. I've barely ever done a still life. And what I really want to paint are portraits."

Another jaw-dropper. Peter had perhaps attempted one portrait in his whole life. Lately, I felt like I hardly knew the man. What I did know was that he was stuck and that I was probably his best bet at getting unstuck, a role I would eventually perfect. I cocked my head to one side, contemplating his position. Like me, Peter had to get up every day to perform a demanding work schedule at a job he couldn't wait to quit and he had all of the responsibilities that came with family, bills and managing a home. On top of this, he had to carve out time and energy for painting and magically pull out his artistic genius each night when he was most exhausted. It was circular and self-defeating. No wonder he couldn't figure out how to get started. That empty canvas probably loomed far larger in his mind than it was in reality.

"Isn't this just about checking technical skill right now?" I asked, trying to return him to the essential point of the exercise. "I know your ultimate aim in all this is to capture the essential beauty of a thing, but for right now, in the fitness stage, paint anything. Copy your favorite artists. Use an old photo."

Layperson though I was, I knew this suggestion was a gross over-simplification but felt it could be excused if he could latch on to even a kernel of it to jumpstart his painting. Frankly, I was less concerned at this moment about *what* he painted than about the fact that he *was painting*. From the spark in his eyes, I saw my little intervention had worked. Peter found his beginning.

The artist didn't notice my departure from the studio that day. In truth, he'd barely have noticed my presence at all had I not spoken, a rare experience with my normally warm and attentive partner. Yet, I was unfazed. My invisibility in this moment was a consequence of his newfound preoccupation, and this made all the difference. His launch meant that the change we craved was in the making and that I was now free to find my own beginning. I wasted no time. Aside from unblocking the artist's psyche and the occasional bank roll, my first undertaking in the five-year fitness plan was to find a new job sufficient to support us where I could be content enough to settle for a long period. I did my best to accelerate the process. In truth, it would have been impossible to do otherwise.

With every day that passed, it became harder to manage my present situation because my heart and mind had already moved on. It was like an out of body experience. Who says you can't live in two alternate dimensions simultaneously? The present was the past. The future was now. I needed to get on with it.

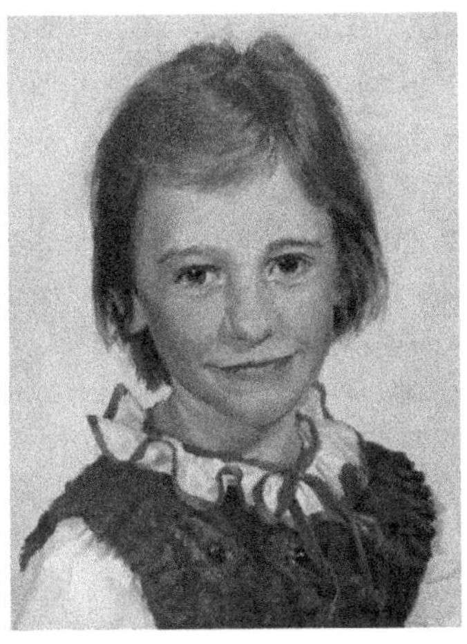

3

The Artist's Study

"Every artist was first an amateur."
—Emerson

In the months that passed after our trip to Nova Scotia, job applications rolled out, and painting attempts began to collect in the studio.

"You're on your way!" I sang out happily to Peter, half skipping up to the easel.

He greeted me with a dampening frown and a face tight with frustration. One look told me that his own optimism was deflating under the pressure of his daily obligations and self-imposed art agenda.

"This is starting to take a toll on you," I observed, "and there is no better way to crush your creativity."

He offered nothing in reply but a blank face. Peter was stuck again. I hesitated for a moment, not certain at this early stage how much to forbear or interfere, a balancing act in any marriage, but this was a new dimension. This was the artistic process, and I was unsure of my ground. Taking cues from the past and crossing my fingers, I opted for a kick-start.

"You're imploding," I declared, grabbing his arm and dragging him outside for a walk. "You need air. So does your work. It's time to get a piece or two finished and out of that studio."

"I'm not ready," he protested aloud, though I'd caught a flicker of recognition of the truth in his eyes.

"Maybe not as ready as you'd like, but just the same, it's time for an unveiling," I insisted. "This will be only a preliminary. You have absolutely nothing to lose," I finished confidently. He shot me an incredulous look, but I had my next arrow ready. "A five-year plan with flexibility means there is room for trial and error."

Click.

He picked up the pace on our return to the house and then hurried into the studio with renewed verve to begin the painting that he would, for the first time since art school, submit to public scrutiny.

"Thanks for getting me back on track," he smiled appreciatively, grabbing his brushes.

In my junior year of college, having taken French since the seventh grade, I went to France to study for a year. I'd been told by teachers that my French was excellent, but this was primarily classroom French. I'd never really had to converse with a native. On my first evening in Paris, impatient to see the city, I dropped my bags in my room and raced out to the streets with some fellow students. We wandered until we were completely and utterly lost. It was a time before smart phones, and we'd left our Michelin guides in the dorm in our haste for a first glimpse of the city. *Oh, God, I'm going to have to ask for directions*, I panicked. And I did. From a Parisian. In flowing French. The fact that years of studying could be called up on demand the instant I needed them was nothing short of miraculous to me.

Now, it was Peter's turn for a miracle. Though he had barely lifted a brush for years, he had spent his down hours voraciously poring over art books and art work since he had left school. Whenever the family visited the library or a bookstore, he made a beeline for the art section and emerged with arms full of material. Out of this latent education materialized his first serious oil painting, a portrait of our daughter.

"What do you think?" he asked as we stood before a Rockwell-esque, head-to-waist portrait based on an old, first-grade school photo.

Our daughter had chosen her favorite ruffled blouse and kelly green sweater-vest for the photo, and the photographer had snapped just in time to memorialize a characteristic smirk on her face. Peter's rendition caught it all.

"I like it," came my unsophisticated reply. Inwardly, I was truly amazed at how well this first portrait had turned out but I had no confidence in my own taste, unschooled as it was.

"Thanks, but does it pass the ultimate portrait test? Does it look like her?" Peter pressed, watching me in earnest. "Does it pass the 'mom' test?"

I tilted my head and looked again at the painting. It did look like our daughter with all her charm and impishness. Peter was encouraged by my reaction and pleased with his first foray, which meant he'd cleared a significant hurdle.

"What we need now is a show," I prompted, still smiling my support to the artist, "to find out what the buying public thinks."

Peter started visibly.

Well done though it was, he had completed only one painting. I knew his line of least resistance would be to remain comfortably in the studio creating a pile of work before he felt confident enough to go public. I also knew that the longer he waited for the fitness test, the harder it would be, and said so. Our joint future direction was, after all, dependent on the outcome.

He did not argue. He exhibited his usual calm demeanor in the face of my suggestion, but we'd been together too long for this to fool me. On the inside, he was doing flips. Whereas I jibber-jabbered my jitters for all to hear, he typically remained silent when stressed and often sank into a funk punctuated by cat naps and bowls of Cheerios.

"OK," he finally agreed.

I eyed him, concerned that I was pushing him too hard.

"Are you sure you're up for this?" I double-checked.

He nodded.

I accepted his answer but knew I'd get a more accurate reading by monitoring the pantry.

There was really no point to Peter's apprehension; I was already tied up in knots on his behalf. This vicarious anxiety only reinforced what I already knew: I could never be an artist in my own right. Lack of skill aside, I can't imagine putting my best effort on display only to have it picked apart by a harsh public. What compels someone to do this for a living? There's an aspect of madness to it…and a great deal of personal courage. If there is any level of artistic success at which the fear of falling short dissipates, I have not seen it. Perhaps this is why artists bond so tightly. I secretly harbored reservations that Peter, who was a deeply feeling person, had the stomach for this gig over the long haul. In an unusual show of self-control, I kept this fear to myself. After all, if I'd voiced every reservation I had about this project, we'd never have got off the beach in Nova Scotia.

"I found a local show!" Peter announced one day as I came through the door.

Through an artist-friend, he'd heard of a regional exhibit that would serve nicely as an early test of his skills. Weeks later, one stomach tight, the other full of Cheerios, we headed for our first art show together as participants. Peter's portrait won first prize! He was naturally pleased about this recognition but more so about the crowd's general response to his work. In fact, he'd watched the crowd more closely than the judge. "The Peoples' Choice Award," he'd confided in the car on the way to the show, "is the only award that really counts. It's the buying public I need to impress."

He knew the limitations of painting from an old photo and he was well acquainted with the prodigious skills of the successful portraitists of the time. Still, he had come to present his first attempt to the public and had prevailed on that point. Far sooner than either of us had expected, he had passed the fitness test.

"Time to reset the five-year plan," he whispered in my ear through an irrepressible grin. "Time for the *skill-building* phase."

The most unexpected outcome of the fitness test had nothing to do with Peter or the portrait. It had to do with me. Formerly content simply to say I "liked" or "did not like" artwork, the competition showed me the ground I needed to cover to truly understand this world Peter was entering. I had got a taste of what I did not know about art which, at that time, could have filled a hard drive. How ironic it was that I, not the artist, was facing a crossroad at this early juncture. I could remain aloof in my easily defined roles of financial backer and motivator. Or, I could become a fully functioning and useful partner who contributed in every possible way to the enterprise. By the time we exited the show, this dilemma had reached full pitch, and I was tight with tension.

In the car, I voiced my quandary aloud in a shaky voice, broaching it timidly at first, not wanting to rain on Peter's parade.

"How would you feel if I learned more about art and the business of art so I could help you more? It would be a way for us to work together like we've always wanted and also for me to be more completely a part of all of this."

I stopped there, choked with uncertainty and not knowing what else to say, anxiously awaiting the verdict.

"ARE YOU KIDDING ME?" he jumped in his seat. "I'd LOVE it!"

Instantly, my tension deflated into a profound relief, proof that this was the outcome I'd really wanted.

And so began my art education. From that point on, I watched every possible paint stroke and soaked up all I could about light, values, perspective and composition. I wheedled my way into Peter's conversations with other artists and listened eagerly to art critiques. I learned about history, media, materials, marketing, taxes, and even the law, taking careful notes to chronicle our combined progress.

"I'm on a mission," I explained to friends and family as I peppered Peter with questions.

If this plan was going to work, I was going to be right there beside him in every possible way, my favorite place to be in the whole world.

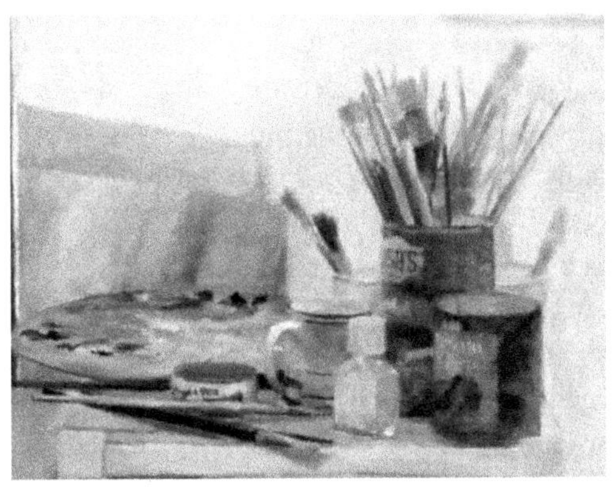

4

A Stroke of a Different Color

"Different strokes for different folks."
—Sly & the Family Stone

Newly vested with a partnership and eager to learn, my first serious art lesson was not actually about art itself; it was about art etiquette. Put more bluntly, I needed to learn how to behave in public.

"God, that's awful," I said aloud to Peter as we strolled through an area art museum, pointing to a generic white plaster head with a bunch of nails pounded into the skull. "How is that art?"

He gently curled my finger back into my hand and, lowering my arm, whispered, "Not so loud. The artist could be within earshot."

My head jerked up, and I scanned the room. I couldn't imagine anyone taking artistic pride in such a piece but I took his point. Outspokenness, however natural, had no place at an art exhibit. I would curb my commentary so as not to subject an artist to the very public criticism I feared for Peter.

"Right," I agreed, then smiled gamely and reasoned, "I'll only keep my negative asides to myself. Any artist would want to hear a compliment."

Peter's portrait of our daughter was not for sale—it would remain a keepsake in the artist's private collection—but money could not have brought more value to the piece. Having won a regional blue ribbon, it was automatically entered into the state competition, where Peter would get double the exposure and feedback. We drove over five hours to experience the exhibit in person.

"I'm going to hang out near the painting to watch the general reaction," he whispered conspiratorially, waving me off to look at the rest of the show.

The portrait received compliments from fellow artists and visitors alike. Peter's resolve was on fire as he took his seat next to me for the presentation of awards.

The show was a mixed media event—sculpture, photographs, textiles and paintings in both realistic and abstract styles—so the judge had our sympathy, having had the difficult job of evaluating apples over oranges. There were some very intricate and well accomplished works that reflected real skill and clearly stood above the others. All but one of these did not place. We sat in curious but courteous silence as awards were distributed to artists whose work reflected much less talent.

When the judge finally introduced the first-place winner, he held up a framed fabric collage that featured a hole in the center of the canvas. Peter and I exchanged quick glances at each other, both recalling my earlier (though discreetly whispered) characterization of this piece as simplistic and crafty rather than skilled and artistic. And, what was with that hole in the middle? The judge, a university professor of art history, had deemed the piece worthy of first prize and was now expounding at length upon his reasons, the thoughtfulness of the design and the artistic excellence that had obviously gone into the work. True to my behavioral reformation, I shifted around in my chair to channel my astonishment, and not a single peep escaped my mouth. Meanwhile, the artist, who'd been seated to Peter's right, climbed the stairs to the stage to receive the judge's accolades and accept her blue ribbon.

After thanking the judge, the winner returned to her seat and received Peter's polite congratulations. She laughed to him, saying loud enough for us both to hear, "This piece is really a mistake. I was cutting out more pieces of fabric to glue on and accidentally poked a hole through the center of the canvas. But I decided to submit it anyway." She laughed again.

I was stunned. A mistake had won first prize? And worse, she couldn't keep that to herself?

My hands gripped the chair, and I stared straight ahead, squeezing my lips tightly together like an offended church lady. I held to my vow of silence, but no words were required to convey the *ARE YOU KIDDING ME?* that I was telepathically beaming to Peter. Just in case, he reached over a knowing, precautionary hand and placed it on my knee. I looked around the room at the other artists whose work was clearly superior and had involved serious intent and technical prowess. I was appalled on their behalf. How did they feel knowing their careful work had taken a second seat to a few rags stuck with glue and embellished by a slip of the scissors? Their polite faces gave me no indication. Art shows, I decided then and there, were a joke. A complete crock.

Back in the car, free to speak my mind, I wondered aloud at Peter's future profession in light of the absurdity we'd just witnessed.

"How can anyone who produces serious work put himself through this?" I demanded to know.

"Not all competitions are like this," he patiently explained. "This judge was a teacher, not an artist himself, and obviously valued the unusual. There will be other venues where I'm judged against my peers by professionals experienced in painting with oils."

How could he be so reasonable while my indignation for him raged on? It took the entire drive home and a long lecture from Peter for me to maturely understand the subjective nature of art appreciation, critique and judging.

"Art is not science. There's no objective measure," he concluded softly.

I looked over and considered him as if for the first time. It was Peter, after all, and not I, who'd just put himself out there. It was he whose work had been deemed unworthy of notice next to a pile of damaged drapery cuttings. If he was unfazed, so should I be.

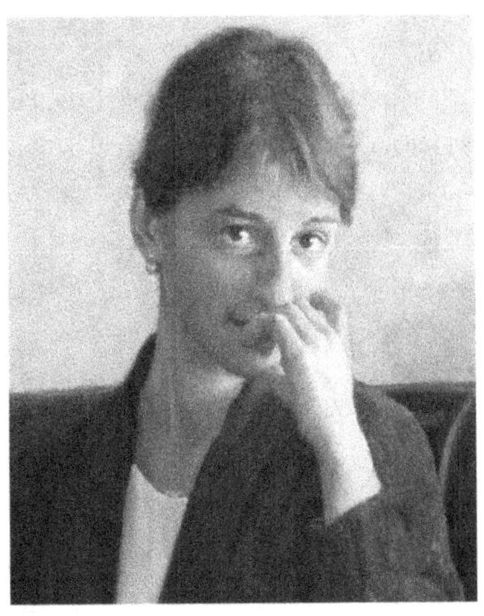

5

A Fresh Canvas

*"Every artist dips his brush in his own soul and
paints his own nature into his pictures."*
— Henry Ward Beecher

On my next visit to the studio, Peter was industriously at work on a huge painting of himself sitting in front of his easel surrounded by studio clutter. His palette was arrayed with color, and he alternated with quick hand movements between several brushes and a palette knife.

"It's inspired by Rockwell's *Triple Self Portrait,*" he explained to me animatedly, jerking his head toward the open book on the floor depicting Rockwell's rendition. "I'm going to call it *Cellar Dweller.* Self-portraits are used by many artists when there is no other subject available."

I noted with amusement that he had decided to pay homage to Rockwell by including the book opened to the *Triple Self Portrait* page in the lower corner of *Cellar Dweller.* "*Cellar Dweller* is the perfect painting for the home page of your new website!" I suggested enthusiastically, pausing for a response.

Without shifting his gaze or even lowering his paintbrush, Peter said, "Sounds good," and pressed on. I did the same. Within a month, I had his website built and activated. The gallery page contained more empty space than paintings, but it was a start.

Not content to rely on a single success, in the year following the state art show, Peter painted a second portrait of our daughter, age 18, this time from life, with photos used only for detail reference. This portrait won first prize and the People's Choice award at the state level.

In the wake of this achievement, the budding artist received several commissions for portraits of children. To my bewilderment, his reaction to the commissions was noticeably restrained.

"What is going on?" I asked uncomprehendingly. "Aren't these commissions good news?"

Learning about art was child's play when compared to keeping pace with the inner workings of the artist.

"Yes, but I'm 50 years old," he spoke to my confusion as he paced the floor. "Will I have time to develop my portrait skills enough to be competitive? I don't know. I'm not connected to the portrait-buying network, and there are so many established artists out there. Will I be able to make it?" he fretted.

Not long after this revelation, I found myself traipsing through historic Boston while Peter attended sessions at a national conference of the Portrait Society of America. Where his self-doubt would lead, whether it would quickly derail his art career or simply change its course, these were the mysteries on which I dwelt as I walked the city. Peter and I caught up at meal times when I listened attentively to his frank and evolving assessment of his skills and the market. The conference, though informative, did not resolve his indecision over portraiture. His vacillation persisted. Unsettling though the uncertainty was, all I could do was be patient and focus on my own role in the five-year plan.

While Peter searched his soul, I was applying for everything that wasn't tied down regardless of geography. Our preferences for the East Coast inevitably crept in. We'd spent our childhoods there and our dating years collecting shells on New Jersey's white beaches. We and our children had been born there. "Oh, what I wouldn't give for the smell of pines and salt water again," I dreamed aloud to Peter. I secretly pinned my hopes on a business management position in North Carolina and, when a similar opportunity opened up in the Midwest, I kept it quiet for a while.

"Remember, we promised we'd do anything for a change," Peter admonished after he discovered the job opening. The universe, too, remembered this pledge, steering us about as far from either coast as we could get. We landed in Omaha, Nebraska. The job itself was fitted to me like a glove and fulfilled my part of the plan, but it would be some time before my imagination let go of the coast and fully embraced Omaha as our new home.

Within weeks of settling into a rented town house, our son and daughter, each now married, relocated to Omaha as well, and both couples temporarily crammed into the little rental with us. To make room for our expanded household, Peter's studio shrank to a corner by a small window in the basement.

"I don't remember all these people being part of our five-year plan," I said, motioning from the couch to our sprawling new housemates.

"You didn't read the fine print. They're covered under Section 2A, the flexibility provision," Peter laughed, shaking his head.

The artist continued to mull over his future prospects. I did not interfere. Not everything fell under the "partnership articles". I gave him plenty of space for self-determination but I also observed him minutely and formed an opinion of my own. Peter naturally started a painting from a feeling about the subject and worked to the outer expression. Even in his early trials, there was always a subtle "something else" underlying the image that reflected his personal connection with the subject, hence his ease painting portraits of our daughter. Painting a person cold or just to please the buyer, it seemed to me, would be incongruous with his nature. I waited and watched for the artist's light-bulb moment, knowing I could have it completely wrong.

Just as he was beginning to wear visible signs of his inner portrait struggle, he received an unusual commission to paint a retirement gift: a still life depicting pieces representative of the recipient's life—his work, family and ancestry. It was the first of its kind for Peter, and he instantly connected with it. Together, we had a great deal of fun identifying symbols to represent the retiree's life and playing creatively with the composition design. Because of the recipient's Dutch lineage, Peter sought a Vermeer-ish look, so the lighting was particularly tricky. We cobbled together a clumsy but functional setup in the rental house basement corner, out of which arose a still life that pleased both painter and buyer. This commissioned "story painting" planted a seed that would germinate in a way the artist never anticipated.

We spent countless Saturdays driving all over the city in search of a permanent home. On one such excursion, Peter steered us through an older neighborhood and abruptly pulled to the side of the road in front of a cozy, 1950's Cape Cod that had clearly been vacant for a while.

"I saw an ad for this one," he explained.

"But it's no longer available," I said, perplexed, and pointed to the sign on the lawn conspicuously labeled "Under Contract".

"I know," Peter answered, "but I'd like to see if the owner, if he's there, will show it anyway. I just like this place."

I scanned the property, unclear what he was seeing. The picket fence, flaked with the remains of white paint, was falling over. The front porch was disintegrating. The siding looked really tired. There were two huge old air conditioners, clearly out of service, hanging precariously from the windows.

I unenthusiastically followed him to the door, which was answered by a friendly man holding a can of spackle. Despite the sign on the lawn, he invited us in. Within minutes, I became a convert. Large country kitchen. Wood floors. Plenty of windows and light filling every room. Big basement. Solid build. Room for everybody. We loved it. Impulsively, I extended my business card to the gracious owner.

"Just in case your deal falls through," I said to him, smiling.

"It's a long shot, I know," I told Peter as we walked to the car, "but you've got to be in it to win it."

Two days later, my phone rang.

"Are you still interested in the house?" the owner asked. "The first buyers withdrew."

I covered the phone to fill Peter in. He leapt up and punched the air. We quickly agreed on a price by phone and gave a resounding Yes! to the owner.

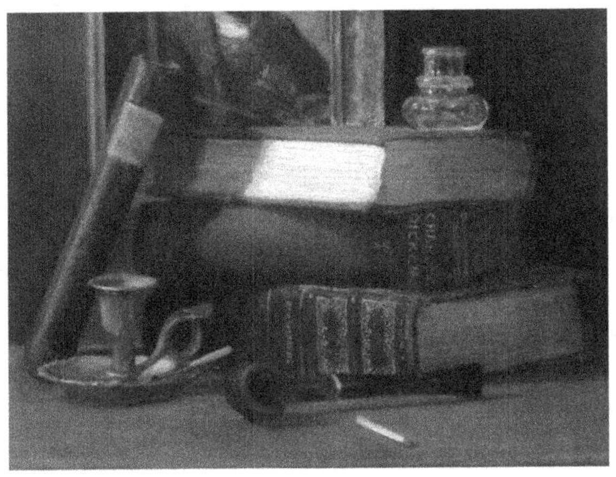

6

Art Council

"Life is a great big canvas; throw all the paint you can at it."
—Danny Kaye

It was sheer joy to me to have our kids back at home, but there was an unanticipated benefit to our full house: Peter was never short of forthright critics or sincere encouragement. Our son and daughter, joined by their new spouses, were very excited about his career change and stepped up to offer a fresh look at his work whenever invited and even when they weren't. The four formed a collaborative support group which Peter dubbed his "Council of Four". The Council took its job seriously and became a regular contributing force to his artistic growth. Our son was the most detailed in his constructive critiques, commenting on sophisticated points like individual brush strokes, composition geometry and unfinished portions of the canvas.

"You're getting washed out right here," he'd say to the artist, whose gentle nature tended toward the subdued. "Don't forget the importance of bold strokes and dark contrasts."

Our daughter focused more on the artist himself and on his

creative process, helping him sustain his optimism, brainstorm ideas and remember the joy of painting. She occasionally picked up a brush herself and worked alongside her father in the studio. As the spouses-in-law gained confidence, they, too, joined in. The Council became increasingly invaluable as the realistic challenges of becoming an accomplished artist began to overtake the romantic notion in Peter.

Around the same time as the Council scattered to their respective new homes, Peter and I moved into the Cape Cod. It was the peak of the housing bubble on the coasts, yet we sold our old home for a decent price and paid reasonably for the new one. Boxes were still scattered throughout the house when I was hurried into the main floor bedroom, now transformed into a studio, where a number of recent paintings were lined up in a row.

"This is my father," he announced animatedly, pulling me over to an arrangement on the table of an old pipe alongside a tea cup that would cry "Dad" to everyone in the family. "Do you see? It's a portrait!" he declared. "Not in the usual sense. This is symbolic, you know, like the commissioned painting. It tells a human story, a narrative, like Rockwell's work. The painting says something more than the sum of its parts."

I saw just what he meant. I picked up a small six-by-eight-inch color sketch of what appeared to be Peter's infamous bedroom laundry pile, a feature of our home over which we frequently had words, and looked over at him quizzically.

"It's me!" he answered excitedly, enjoying his own humor.

"And this one?" I asked, pointing to a beautiful composition he'd set up in front of the easel with my favorite pale yellow pitcher and a green bowl filled with fresh apples on a lace table cover.

He turned to me, smiling warmly.

"Pale yellow is your color, you know—soft—and the fruit reminds me of your wholesomeness, your gardening and cooking," he explained. "I'm going to add the morning light and the sense of stillness that you love." He paused, then added simply, "It's you."

I melted on the spot, incredulous not only that he saw all these things in me but that he could represent them so masterfully. Then, I went right to the kitchen to reserve a space on the wall, smiling in the realization that Peter was painting portraits after all.

The energizing effect of Peter's *Great Portrait Epiphany* was hard to miss as he tackled still life painting after painting in his quest for technique, quality and control. He experimented with composition, pre-toned panels, tools to check perspective and creative backgrounds. He grappled with the subjective side of negative space, point of view and overall abstract form. He began gradually to shift away from photo references to painting from the real thing. Above all other subjects, flowers emerged as his first love, and I was happy to oblige him by planting extensive flower beds all around the new house.

"Lesson for the day," he laughed, indicating a vase with a drooping bouquet. "Paint the flowers first."

At this early stage, he was learning so fast and improving so quickly that it was hard to hold it all in his head.

"You forgot to use your T square," I reminded him one evening as I eyeballed a recent study, tilting my head to synchronize my line of sight with the leaning vase.

"Yeah, I guess it's a little off," he admitted, "but you know I have a brain leakage problem."

We both laughed, as I understood his meaning: I was the embodiment of the mental checklist; Peter was the antithesis. "I can only hold three ideas at a time," he'd claim, laughing heartily to me and the Council. "If you give me a fourth, one of the other three will drop off." This was a great source of family humor but an impediment in the studio. I encouraged the artist to write things down, spouting the virtues of written checklists as a cure for everything from marital spats (You forgot to buy milk again) to insomnia (Write it down and clear your mind). In all fairness, he did try.

"You made a note about the T square. Where's the checklist we created with the Council last week…the one on yellow paper?" I asked, rummaging around the studio.

"It should be right there," he said, busying himself with the re-arrangement of his still life.

"Where? I'm not finding the yellow pad."

"Oh, yeah, well," he reached over to grab a slip of paper, "I actually lost the first one and re-wrote what I could remember, but now…"

"Let me guess. You can't read your own notes."

"Yeah, and it takes me too long to type."

Peter could command a paint brush but had never got awards for penmanship. And he was a graduate of the henpecking typing school. Grabbing the list, I disappeared from the studio and returned shortly with a neatly typed list, which I tacked to the top of his easel post.

"Let's see if this method works," I said sympathetically, still feeling that, given the choice, I'd have taken his creativity over my hyper-organization in a heartbeat.

That very organization and its adjunct, the critical eye, began to detect some strange occurrences around the house. My conch shells disappeared from the bathroom shelf. Bookshelves were disheveled. Dishes on the hutch were rearranged. I came up short in the kitchen.

"Where are the apples we just bought?" I asked, pointing to the empty fruit bowl.

"Oh, sorry," Peter confessed, sincerely contrite, and then quickly left to retrieve the remains from the studio.

I followed him and discovered not only apples but the missing dinner candles, a variety of tea cups and saucers, the vinegar and oil decanters, several books I had been reading, and my favorite vase.

Everyday matter—what a French art acquaintance would later refer to as "quotidien"— fascinated Peter, and he began churning out little paintings of common objects from our own stores. With traditional portraits, he had struggled for practice subject matter. Not so with story portraits and their natural by-product, the still life. Dishes. Cookies. Candy dishes. Jelly jars. Breakfast plates. Crayons. Even soap in the soap dish.

"You are NOT taking those to the studio," I said firmly as I caught him stealing freshly baked rolls from the counter.

The artist had turned raider, but at least I could take comfort that I knew where he kept his stash. By now, the studio had become gloriously littered with dead flowers, old food and knick-knacks. Still life and story portrait attempts lay everywhere.

"I see you hit the thrift store again," I observed with a sigh of resignation. "Just what we need. More stuff."

He grinned so infectiously, it was hard not to join him. On my way out, I spied a newly acquired pair of cobalt blue mugs.

"Oh, just the thing for the kitchen," I said, swooping them up without compunction.

"Is it me, or have you found your first calling?" I asked when I caught him sneaking my favorite teapot and basket from the kitchen.

He smiled a Mona Lisa smile and slipped mysteriously into the studio.

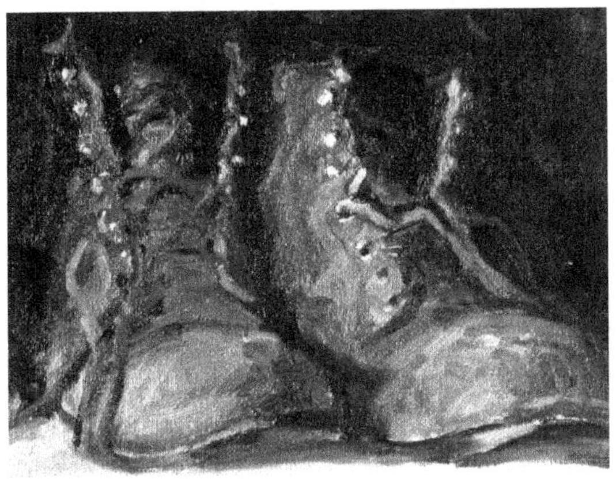

7

Perspective

"You must look within for value but must look beyond for perspective."
—Denis Waitley

Almost a year had passed to the day since we'd moved into the Cape Cod. I plodded contentedly to my new job every day, and Peter, artist by night and weekend, continued working at his engineering job, traveling four out of five week days across five states. His schedule was grueling, and the competing demands of the old profession and the new were a source of increasing tension.

"You seem to start preparing for Monday earlier and earlier every weekend," I observed one Sunday morning when he'd quit the studio before lunch.

"It sucks more and more energy and takes more and more willpower as the weeks wear on," he said. "I can't concentrate. I've got the usual dull meetings to look forward to all day tomorrow," he complained wearily, "and more pressure about deadlines and quotas."

His inner struggle was more intense than I'd ever seen it, and he fidgeted and writhed in his seat as on the rare occasions when he wore a suit and tie, as if his clothes were physically strangling him.

"Only four more months," I said reassuringly, "and then we can plan your exit."

I perceived his discomfort, and eyed him nervously, still clinging to the hope that he'd hold out until the end of the year when we could be in a better place financially for him to quit. His anticipated defection from engineering would reduce our income by half and make me the sole breadwinner until the art began to sell. We were prepared to live modestly, but I hoped to clear some obligations before the new life began.

He wordlessly rose, walked over and sat next to me on the couch. His soft blue eyes were doing all the talking. *I want out,* they told me. I drew in my breath to argue that we weren't ready, that he should stick it out for a bit longer, but the pain of the conflict inside him was just too acute to dismiss. He'd had enough, and I knew it. I got up and slid into the desk chair in front of the computer, then turned to him.

"What do you want to say in your resignation?"

He choked, jumped up and gave me a long hug, the kind that says everything when words cannot.

"Are you sure?" he asked searchingly.

"It's time," I said determinedly, my heart pounding violently in silent protest.

What difference would a few paychecks really make in the long run? Whatever it was, we'd deal with it. We worked together on the letter and, by the time Peter added his signature, my doubts had been put in their proper place, and my heart had resumed its normal rhythm. This decision was long overdue.

In twenty-four hours' time, Peter returned from work relieved, elated and as energized as I'd seen him in years. Just two weeks later, engineering was history, and he awoke for the first time as an artist. Not that he called himself an artist. Not yet, though I saw him as one. He was up with his internal clock as usual, fully dressed, though in old jeans and a flannel shirt. The morning had all the outward signs of being no different than any other work day. I studied him closely as I chewed my toast.

"You have that deer-in-the-headlights look on your face, you know," I observed with a smirk. Grabbing my last swallow of coffee, I said softly. "Look, your life has just taken a sharp turn. It's a shock to your senses. You're going to feel off-kilter in the beginning until your inner compass resets and you find your new rhythm. This is going to take time."

He nodded vaguely.

"I guess you're right but I feel like a boy who's skipping school. Shouldn't I be at a meeting somewhere?"

I laughed with him.

"One foot in front of the other, and it'll come to you," I said reassuringly, kissing him on the forehead and grabbing my keys.

Another partner might have spent the drive to work worrying. Not me. Our marriage had long been characterized by taking calculated leaps, and we'd spent several years laying the groundwork for this one. In my book, the leap alone was an accomplishment worth celebration. I calmly turned the ignition, blew a kiss to the face in the window and pulled out.

He saw me off to work with a final look of uncertainty, then turned in complete solitude to begin his new venture. Liberated though he was from electrical designs and codes, his state was hardly one of ease or complacency. He'd been waking up every day for 28 years knowing exactly what he had to do. Art may have been his hidden love, but engineering was his comfort zone. The focus, commitment and determination that he'd developed in all those years to provide financially for the household did not just dissipate into paint fumes because he had exchanged his hard hat for a paint brush. These forces would tug at him distractively for a while and add resistance to his transition until he figured out how to redirect his full energy to art. Change really is, at least in part, a matter of physics.

At dinner that evening, Peter voiced his discomfort.

"I feel like I've forgotten something, like I can't be off the hook just like that," he said with a snap of his fingers, a very telling gesture for this gentle man. He stood up and began pacing. "I could hardly concentrate all day. I mostly puttered," he added in a tone of self-reproach. Leaning against the kitchen counter, he crossed his arms over his chest and looked over at me almost apologetically.

I studied him carefully, working to glean from his words and body language the real key to his inner turmoil, aside from monumental change, that is. True, the risk and uncertainty of this undertaking were great in his mind. True, he felt overwhelmed by what lay ahead. But there was something else that night. Peter felt guilty, guilty that his day had produced nothing he could "show-and-tell" as proof that his time at home while I worked at the office had been well spent. The Great Provider in him was asserting itself. We needed to nip this emotional nosedive in the bud or he'd never dig himself out of it.

Watching his face in the window as I'd pulled away that morning, I had known that, for him, the day would be less a celebration than a struggle. In fact, I suspected that months would go by before he fully assimilated his change of profession. He wasn't on vacation. His boss wasn't going to call. He could miss the mandatory meetings today, next week and the week after that. His dream was poised to become reality. Yet, here we were, just eight hours in, and the whole undertaking was in jeopardy not because of the challenge itself but due to his uneasiness with our respective places in the five-year plan.

"I took this on with my eyes open," I said firmly, rising from my chair to add emphasis to the point. "I already had ten years home doing everything I loved while you commuted every day, remember?" I waited for his reluctant grunt of acknowledgment of the ten glorious and fulfilling years I'd worked at home, caring for the farm, volunteering, getting my master's degree and homeschooling our kids. "It's *your* turn now. After you're home for ten years doing what you love, and we're even, we'll talk about what else is to be done."

There was an unquestionable tone of finality in my voice. I assumed my best she-shall-not-be-moved posture and stood waiting and watching Peter's face while he digested this tough love. Everything I'd said was true, but I needed him to know more than that. I needed him to know that, despite the flexibility provision, this particular aspect of the plan was non-negotiable. Otherwise, his progress would always be tentative, and he'd dissipate energy constantly looking over his shoulder for other responsibilities. He had to allow me to be the sole provider for a while. The old life had to give way entirely for the artist to be born.

I thought I caught the split-second when his mind swallowed that difficult pill. After a few moments of silence, he offered, "I'll take care of things around the house like you did for me. It took so much stress off me to have you home."

I threw my arms around his neck.

"Now that we've settled that, want to revamp our five-year plan after supper?" I invited. "It's time to reset the clock and shift from part-time skill-building to full blown professional art school."

His head jerked up in real interest. I knew I had his attention, but it wasn't until months later, when I caught sight of a small painting of his worn-out engineering work boots entitled *Gave Up the Day Job,* that I knew the artist was really going to be alright.

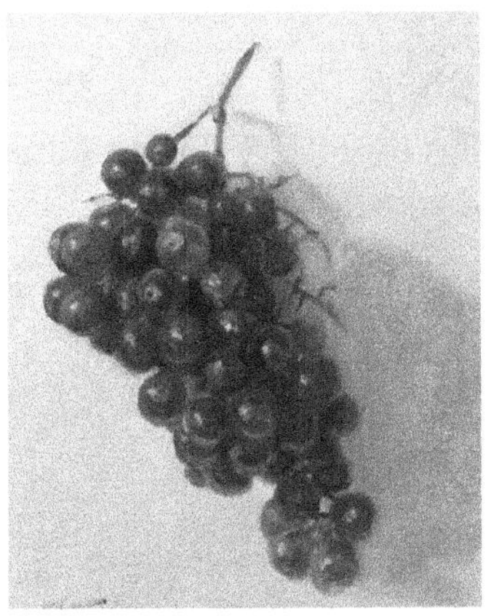

8

Stretching the Canvas

*"I find painting a much slower process than comedy,
where you can go a mile a minute verbally and hope to God
that some of the people out there understand you."*
—Jonathan Winters

By this time, I had already filled several notebooks with notes about art and anecdotes about the artist (and his partner) from both in front of and behind the canvas. Looking back through my scribbling helped me to sort through and make sense of our experiences.

"I know I'm only working with one artist," I told the Council of Four as I flipped the pages, "but I've collected a lot of useful information, and mine is a very intimate perspective."

If nothing else, I reasoned to myself, smoothing out a crisp new page, writing was fun and a great excuse to revisit the stationery store.

Unlike my writing preoccupation, Peter's plunge into professional art school did not enhance his clarity. On the contrary, his palette and canvases continued to be inconsistent and exploratory as he pushed for breakthroughs in technique and style. Experimentation was the order of the day, and his strain was almost audible, like the creak of a tree bending from the weight of a heavy snow. However well-intentioned his attempts in the secluded studio, however, they were not enough.

"You're getting loopy alone in that studio day after day," I nudged him. "You're living like a hermit. You need to get out. You need feedback from other artists, not just from me and the Council of Four."

He was struggling to find his place in the art world, to determine what to paint and how to paint it. To accomplish this, much as the introvert hated to admit it, he needed peers. Not all of an artist's striving is confined to the actual canvas.

Before we'd moved to Omaha in 2004, Peter had met Darren Mauer, a professional oil painter who'd become a great friend and advisor. Peter had never been loquacious, but art loosened his tongue, and he and Darren could talk for hours.

"Maybe there's a Darren or two in Omaha," I suggested.

He scoured Nebraska for kindred spirits and, to my relief, found a few. He also searched the internet and found dozens. It wasn't that he hadn't used the internet before. He had a web site, after all. He'd found his engineering job and our former house online. Not until this moment, though, had he fully apprehended the breadth of art resources on the young but rapidly expanding worldwide web. And not until he made these contacts did I realize that I'd been holding my breath out of concern over his isolation.

At Darren's suggestion, Peter looked particularly into art blogs and was immediately impressed.

"Blogs are where the action is," he told me with an excitement so palpable that my spine tingled. "I'm following all these," he said and scrolled through links to artists whom he hoped to emulate in style, proficiency or genius.

So inspired was Peter that he was soon happily posting works-in-process on his own blog, *Daily Painting Practice,* and gathering interested followers—friends, family, enthusiasts, artists and even potential buyers. I checked the blog from work whenever I could to stay in touch with his progress.

It was amazing how quickly, after his first post in July, 2006, his connections mushroomed and the value of the blog multiplied. Here, Peter found stimulation, challenge, discourse and an international network of empathetic and constructive critics without the necessity of leaving his studio. And posting had the added benefit of artistic catharsis, clearing the way for new painting attempts, and not only relieving his partner from counseling duty, but freeing the artist to turn supporter in his own right.

Nothing can take the place of working elbow to elbow with your peers (not even a devoted partner), but for a budding artist trying to break into a new world, this online network was priceless. Within 30 days, *Daily Painting Practice* was visited by thousands of viewers including artists from 31 countries whose substantive commentaries were material to Peter's progress and morale. It wasn't quite like the megahits we see on social media today, but for its time, it was significant.

The irony of Peter's rapid expansion to digital relationships did not escape us…or our son. Peter and I are of the generation born to black rotary phones and now (with mixed emotions) stuffing cell phones into our pockets. We have the fading perspective of having lived quite comfortably detached from electronics and to this day prefer personal visits and handwritten letters to digital voice, video and text. Our son, by contrast, from the moment he came in contact with a touch screen in preschool, has lived and breathed technology as if he was born with little nano chips in his bloodstream.

"I can't believe how many artists I've met." The new blogger extolled the virtues of the internet one weekend, waving his arms expansively. "I'm learning so much from these people."

Our son was graciously forbearing and offered both encouragement and suggestions, though his eyes shone brightly and, once or twice, I caught the corner of his mouth twitching.

Networking became especially advantageous as Peter reached for a style of his own. Early in the game, he had made two important decisions. Abstract painting, though alluring for its monetary promise, held no appeal.

"How do abstract artists know if they're getting better?" he would ask as he worked canvas after canvas in pursuit of technical control.

Nor was he drawn to hyper-realism.

"The talent is admirable," he'd say, "but for me, the painting is too close and tight like a photo. I want more expression."

"You seem clear about what you *don't* want, in broad strokes anyway," I summarized for him. "But what is it you *do* want?"

Therein lay the $64,000—scratch that—$1,000—no, at Peter's going prices, it was more like a $150 question. He began posting his experiments online just to see how they played to the public. Initially, he emulated old masters: Rembrandt's classic lighting, Vermeer's subtlety, Rockwell's strength of composition, van Gogh's boldness, Monet's and Renoir's expressive hues, Homer's sense of place, Fantin Latour's simple backgrounds. Peter marveled at the quality of their work, especially as most pieces had been achieved without the luxuries of heat, artificial lighting and today's commercial paints. The confidence he detected in their strokes was very appealing to him, an emerging artist without a style of his own. Ghosts of the past dominated the studio for some time, but thanks to the internet, the influence of contemporary artists was gaining rapidly.

Style, that alluring brass ring, was forced to take a back seat to a more immediate priority: production. As much due to inexperience as to low confidence, Peter's painting was painfully slow. Though he could complete a painting in a day, he took six to eight hours to finish a small six-by-eight-inch or eight-by-eight-inch canvas board. Inspired by Julian Merrow-Smith's *Postcards from Provence,* and with Darren's help and encouragement, he began to post these little works on his blog using eBay's auction feature to offer them for sale.

"Even if it takes me all day to paint one," he reasoned to me, "the cost to create and ship an unframed piece on small canvas board is really low. Selling a piece for $150 is lucrative."

Sales began to mount, Peter's skills improved, his peer collaboration expanded, and his expenses were covered—a collectively seductive combination that fed both Peter and me in every sense of the word for many months. He became so enamored with this scheme that, in time, he instigated the formation of the *Daily Painters Guild*, a collaborative group of committed and talented daily painters who specialized in small works.

The daily painting formula was so successful and enjoyable that Peter looked askance at anything else. I stepped back as he rode this wave, waiting to see if he'd settle into it permanently.

"You haven't touched your larger canvases," I observed one night, nodding toward a short stack still sealed in plastic in the corner of the studio.

"No."

He waved them off distractedly as he worked the final touches on another loosely-styled little still life.

Out of respect for his energy and focus, I accepted his non-response but threw back at him as I left the studio, "You have paint on your nose, you know."

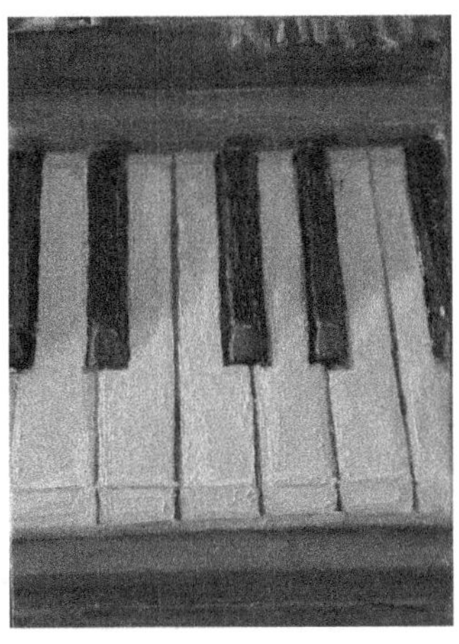

9

Red and Green

If I was really honest with myself at this point, my own palette was turning a tinge of green. It wasn't a full-blown jealousy—more of a longing, actually. I was the one who analyzed, organized and structured things. I set goals. I made things happen. I'd made great use of these talents at work and at home. Yet, I still carried the lingering imprint of my ten-year sabbatical when my creativity could run unleashed. I had never been an artist, but I had home-schooled with an eclectic, out-of-the-box kind of flair, whipped up original masterpieces in the kitchen, made up songs and infused stories with humor. Now, with most of my energies directed toward my jobs, the office and the art partnership, my own creative brushes largely sat for long hours in the turps jar waiting for me to squeeze out a window of downtime.

Yet, it was more than that.

"I wish I had my own calling," I told Peter dispiritedly at

Saturday breakfast, conscious that every muscle in my body was tight with concentration. "I mean outside of supporting our art plan, of course," I was quick to clarify my meaning. "I love working in the art world with you, and my role in your career gives me purpose within its boundaries, but I want something that's mine, something creative that I can build on in my free time."

"I know what you mean," he answered, empathy written all over his face. "It'll come to you. Just keep reaching and give it time."

I studied him for a few moments, processing his instinctual attempt at balance. Peter and I were complements, yes, but there had always been some degree of interplay, a sort of shifting in and out of our respective places according to the need of the moment. Taken alone, we were polar opposites, but placed side by side, we were a human equivalent of what artists call "simultaneous contrast", when two distinct colors on a canvas appear differently together than when standing alone.

"Do you remember van Gogh's *The Night Café in Arles*?" I asked.

"Oh, yeah, I remember everything van Gogh painted," he replied, clearly taken aback, "but I didn't realize you knew that one."

I disregarded the last comment, and opened his van Gogh book to the café painting.

"Well, look at his brilliant reds and greens. They are so distinct and create such contrast in that painting, yet together, they are so vibrant that your eyes have to shift back and forth between the two to take it all in. That's you and me. We are so different but so entwined. I love that we work so well together but I feel lately like the lines between us are getting too blurry. I wonder which is which, red or green, you or me. I've never been defined by my work at the office and, in art, I'm following your lead. Where am *I* in all this?" I asked painfully, then quickly added, "Don't worry. I'm not unhappy. Just searching."

No doubt, I was on my way to becoming an artist without holding a brush, studying the masters, developing my own taste and learning technique through Peter and the people he met. My eye was increasingly more sophisticated, and I was beginning to differentiate between styles, light play and quality down to the brush stroke. I was formulating my own opinions. I could even roughly outline the stages of a painting. The closest I'd ever come before to this level of artistic understanding had been through playing the piano—interpreting music, drilling for technique, practicing eye-hand coordination and understanding the masters. Getting this involved in Peter's dream was bound to mix our colors to some degree, but while I was happy working at his side, I didn't want to lose my own color in his.

Later in the day, he was hard at work on his blog, cutting, pasting and drafting comments. He was so energized and self-reliant in the process that I suddenly appreciated how much his blog success had freed me up.

Leaning in to volunteer some spelling corrections, I said, "You know, your blog could make a great instruction book someday, like how to develop a painting or even how to develop in the art profession."

He sat very still for a moment, then turned to me with a knowing expression.

"I'm the painter, not the writer, in the family. You're the writer."

My heart leapt. I ran for my journal.

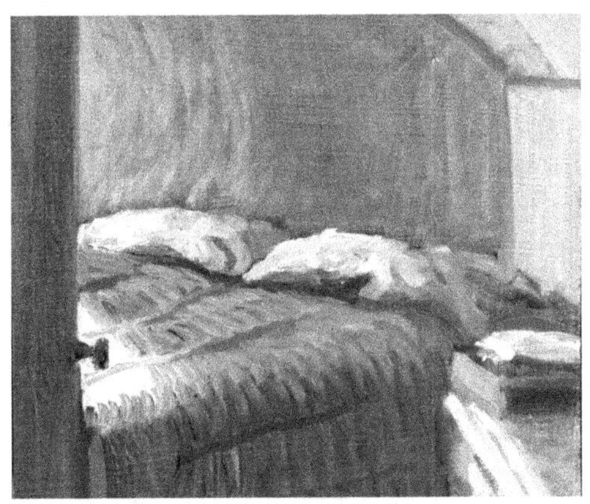

10

Changing Values

"I wanted to paint a picture someday that people would stand before and forget that it was made of paint."
—O. Henry

"Did you catch today's blog post?" Peter asked as I came in the door and, not waiting for an answer, he handed me a small painting he'd finished that morning reminiscent of Vincent van Gogh's *Bedroom in Arles—Sunlight on a Blue Bed.*

Although not a hard core van Gogh fan myself, I could not resist sharing his enthusiasm of the moment. I went upstairs to change and returned for dinner grateful for the segue this painting had provided into what I wanted to say. Pressing him, as I was about to do, was a delicate business if I wanted to motivate him rather than derail his progress. Leaving my food untouched, I cleared my throat, swallowed and slowly began.

"I've been thinking about this for some time." I attempted to keep my speech calm and level. "You've been experimenting and copying so many good artists but you really will eventually have to decide on a style of your own. A consistent style will brand your work. It's how you make a name for yourself."

The age-old forces of pragmatism and artistic expression stared at one another across the table. My chest constricted.

"I love van Gogh," Peter threw back in an uncharacteristically loud and defensive tone as he shifted uncomfortably in his chair. "The confidence of his paint strokes. His color."

I winced, but we'd been married too long for me not to recognize a diversionary tactic when I heard one. He did not like to be pinned down. Who does? It's so…final.

"Yes, I know you do," I said earnestly. "Still, of all the paintings you've done so far, only a handful have actually been in van Gogh's style. You seem to naturally gravitate to a soft kind of realism."

A heavy silence hung over the table in the wake of this declaration. He could not refute it; I had done the math. But my heart beat skittishly nonetheless.

"I don't want to settle," he declared flatly, flushing with internal struggle.

"Try to think of it not so much as settling as striving toward something," I countered as gently as I could. "Style is a dynamic thing, always undergoing refinement. Go for van Gogh-ish, if that's what you truly want. But, sooner rather than later, you must choose an intentional direction out of which will emerge your own signature style."

I let the subject drop on this serious note. It was his choice. All I could do was wait.

Style is pivotal. It'll determine if he stays an amateur painter or becomes a consummate professional, I further argued to myself that night as I recorded our conversation into my journal. I hadn't been the first to introduce the idea, after all. Peter had already heard the truth of it from other artists but he also acutely apprehended the pressure he would feel making the shift from experimentation to consistent delivery.

I watched him closely each time he pulled out a new canvas. He poked at the style beast in every way possible to tease progress from it, which meant, largely, that he just kept on painting. I had to give him points for bravery. He played with undercoating, backgrounds and his palette knife. He accepted dares from the Council of Four to paint subject matter he'd never before attempted. I settled back knowing the style seed had been planted and, if Peter remained true to form, a seedling would inevitably emerge.

In the meantime, he was breaking through something other than style. I'd sensed it immediately when he'd put *Sunlight on a Blue Bed* into my hands. Turning to van Gogh, his usual refuge when he was dealing with uncertainty, was the tip-off. "I'm comfortable with van Gogh," he'd told me time and again. "He helps me loosen up."

"What was going on that you needed Vincent today?" I asked as he cleaned his palette before bed.

"I just couldn't think of anything to paint in here," he told me, waving his hand to indicate the studio.

I scanned the abundant reference material stacked and scattered all over the room. Simple still lifes alone were apparently no longer enough to hold the artist's interest.

"I've been looking online at the things other artists are painting. I need more complexity in my subject matter," he continued.

Ah. The proverbial light bulb flashed in my head.

"So, this is why you actually left the studio for the first time to paint our guest bedroom!" I said brightly, looking with renewed interest and greater understanding at *Sunlight on a Blue Bed.*

Here was a breakthrough, however insignificant it might appear to the outsider. Peter had never before left the studio to paint.

After his inauguration with Vincent, he began to churn out scene after scene of our home—kitchen table, rocking chair, cluttered countertop, piano. He called them "interiors" and posted them on his blog. He even painted a kitchen nocturne. I visited the blog one day at work and found a painting of the entire contents of our pantry.

"If you keep posting scenes of our house," I warned him over the phone, "the whole world is going to know every detail of our life. They've already seen your laundry and know everything we own and eat!"

I needn't have worried about the invasion of privacy. The artist very quickly ran out of steam inside and shifted from interiors to exteriors. If leaving the studio was a step forward, graduating to exteriors was a giant leap. The idea of painting outdoors where he could be seen by others had always been terrifying to him. The first few exteriors were merely outside views through the windows. Next, he painted in the back yard and then in the neighborhood at large. The quotidian aspect never left his painting. Small canvases of old cars, garbage cans, clotheslines, flowering bushes and lawn chairs began to line up on the studio wall. I practically danced with delight as I walked the row of new paintings.

I eyed him curiously.

"I thought you didn't like painting outside."

He shrugged indifferently.

"I just stand where no one can see me."

Inwardly, I giggled at the idea that hiding was his coping strategy. My gaze landed on one particular canvas at the end of the row, and my face screwed up in disgust.

"What is that?"

"It's a bird," he replied matter-of-factly.

"It's a dirty bird," came my far too frank rejoinder, "in the gutter with trash. Ugh. Where's the beauty in that?"

At the sight of this little painting, a warning light had gone off in my head, and it was flashing furiously. Peter had always maintained that his driving purpose for painting was to capture beauty. This bird was something else, an oddity. It seemed to me that, if left unchecked, Peter might detour down the path of the bizarre and peculiar and lose valuable time before he remembered his original underlying intention. I didn't think calling this out was too harsh.

Art associates were always advising Peter to settle down, to find a niche like flowers or fruit to paint exclusively to earn a name for himself. His weakness and his strength, depending on your point of view, were that he was open to painting everything. He didn't want to settle, feeling it would make him stale and bored. With the exception of the filthy avian in the garbage pile, I didn't want that for him either.

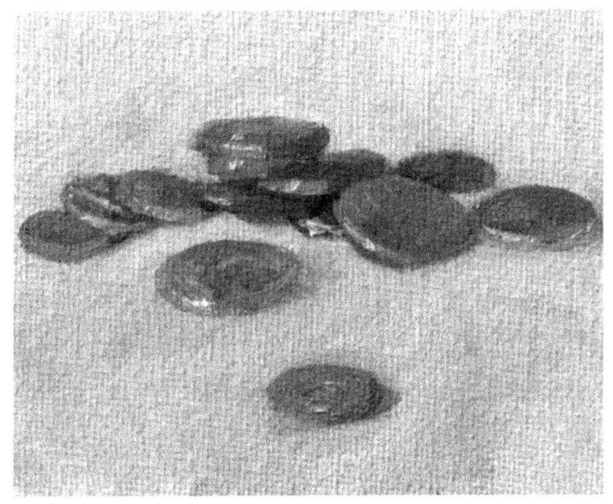

11

The Business of Art

"Money is not the only answer but it makes a difference."
—Barack Obama

"Here's another article telling artists they can turn their love of art into a lucrative venture overnight as if 'You, too, can make a million dollars!'"

I laughed. Peter rolled his eyes. Even with his daily painting success, it was clear that taking the artist from rags to riches or even to a steady income stream took far more than passion. It took business skills. Fortunately, this was something we did not have to learn entirely from scratch, though despite my years in business finance and operations, we were not in a position to be smug. Art is a world unto itself.

My grandmother grew up speaking only German until the First World War when all German was suppressed in favor of English to prove one's patriotism. As a consequence, she forgot German with the exception of one remnant of her girlhood, mispronounced and delivered with a rueful shake of the head, that I later figured out to be "solches Geschäft". Such a business. As Peter and I grappled with the frustrations of the art business, solches Geschäft seemed a fitting oath.

With my background, the Geschäft side naturally fell to me, at least initially. Early on, Peter thought of his art, from a financial standpoint, as a hobby. In fairness, he'd always collected a salary, so selling his creations felt more like play money. "I sold a painting!" he'd announce gleefully, then march off to buy more supplies or reference materials with the proceeds and, if there was any change, to grab a burger and fries on the way home. How do you train a man in profit and loss when he thinks in terms of the cash jingling in his pocket? This was my challenge, and I set about it systematically, so that he actually learned rather than just having it done for him.

"If you think of your art as a business, it's a business," I parroted our CPA's advice, "and, there are limits on the hobby classification. You need to understand what's going on and why," I urged seriously, then broke into laughter at his light-hearted grimaces.

"I get it," he assured me. "You learn art. I learn finance. It's more than fair. You can't just focus on me. You have to have time to relax and garden and read and...," he added the magic words, "to write."

A huge sigh escaped from my chest.

Peter was what I teasingly called detail-challenged, a handicap that had surfaced early in our marriage when I found him rummaging all over our apartment.

"What are you looking for?" I'd asked.

"I can't find my keys."

I'd joined the search that morning. And the next. By the end of our first few weeks together, we had spent four mornings out of five looking for his keys or wallet or glasses.

One evening, at the sound of Peter's footsteps on the stairs, I positioned myself behind the apartment door, hands on my hips in one of those womanly something-has-to-change attitudes. When he swung the door open, I sang out, "Please stop!" He halted on the threshold, eyes twinkling with good humor in anticipation of whatever was to follow. Grinning and pointing to a small basket I'd newly hung on the doorknob, I said in my best flight-attendant voice, "As soon as you come home, put everything in there."

"Great idea," he said, relieved as I was for an alternative to the daily search-and-find method.

It took about a week of practice, but we never spent another morning stressing over lost valuables. (And to this day, we have baskets on our doorknobs.) This was proof positive that we are not destined to remain victims of our natures. Imaginative minds can, in fact, master mundane details. To help Peter learn business management, I planned to capitalize on just that.

To coincide with an exhibition, he decided to purchase an advertisement in *American Art Collector* magazine. I began the ad design but could not find the painting he had in mind to insert. The volume of images on our computer was incredible, as if they'd been breeding amok on the hard drive. What was worse, they were in a state of total chaos. Solches Geschäft. After tedious hours of re-labeling and cataloging photographs, I found the painting for the advertisement, completed the ad, then breathed over Peter's shoulder like a she-dragon to make sure he followed the new system.

"The quality is in the details here as much as in any painting," I asserted. "Efficiencies on the business side leave more room for the creative side."

I looked sideways at him to see if he'd buy this argument. He did.

Cataloging jpegs, collecting receipts, recording mileage, filing taxes—the art Geschäft was a beast that required constant feeding. I created systems and templates so Peter could more easily learn and participate first-hand.

"You can't afford to be sloppy or vague about your business," I preached. "It won't make things better; it'll just leave you in the dark. That's a worse place to be."

It was pretty left-brained stuff, all this tracking and calculating, definitely not Peter's comfort zone, yet he stuck to it and defied the stereotype that artists are bad with finances. Soon, we were reviewing figures together, discussing tax implications, and projecting sales over a candlelight dinner. There's nothing like an Excel spreadsheet for romance. Peter came to understand money just fine and, more importantly, he learned to manage it. It did not interfere with his creativity. It did not slow his production. Quite the contrary, understanding exactly where he stood financially gave him motivation in the right direction.

Geschäft aside, I have often envied Peter's innate obliviousness to the small stuff. He has an incredible ability to "launch", as the Council of Four called it. Give him the spark of an idea, and his expansive mind takes off in pursuit, leaving the present reality behind. Entire conversations have been lost as I have chatted away, his eyes open and looking right at me, his mind entirely in the ethers expanding on something I'd said in the first sentence. "What's the last thing I said?" I'd ask him, rolling my eyes. He'd blink a few times, then come in for a crash landing.

Contrary as it may be to business discipline, the ability to drop everything to chase an idea is an enviable talent and of real value in art. The more closely we've worked, the more I have come to appreciate this just as Peter has admired my own skills, and we've each striven to assimilate some of the other's strengths. Though I've never come close to launching Peter-style, he has taught me to dream, to play with color and to take naps. In the world of Geschäfts, you would say he and I are the ultimate merger.

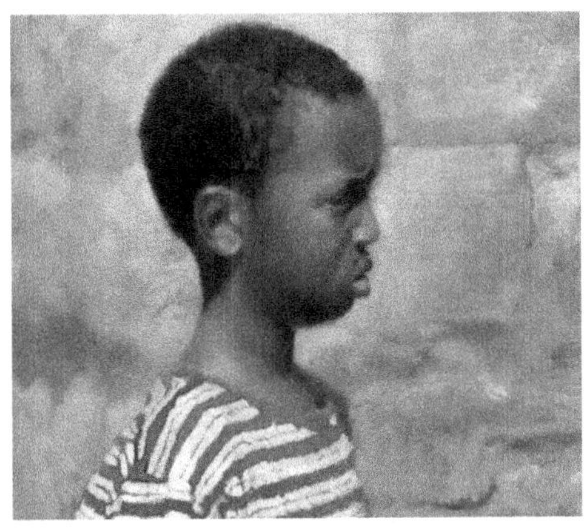

12

Daily Painting Practice

"All I have to do is to work on transition and technique."
—Usain Bolt

If I'd depicted Peter's progress to date in an Excel graph, the overall trend line would reflect gradual improvement, but the graph line itself would peak and valley like alligator teeth. Whenever he hit a low point, he inevitably reviewed his blog comments and daily painting sales for a confidence boost.

Darren visited one weekend, and he and Peter were justly celebrating their respective successes.

"Darren just bought a car with his daily painting earnings!" Peter announced excitedly as I joined them in the living room.

"Wow," I smiled over to Darren. "Congratulations!" This was quite an achievement. Happy as I felt for Darren, I had my reservations about Peter. Despite the respectable earnings and blog following, I felt there was more to his artistic future than small works, and I said so.

"Don't you want to move into larger compositions and get off eBay into galleries?" I challenged him. "Daily paintings are a great niche, obviously rewarding and lucrative, but I don't think you will be happy sticking primarily to tiny canvases long term."

Darren and Peter both energetically countered the point, so I let the matter drop and left them to continue the debate between themselves.

I did not have to revisit the argument. Without further prodding, a nine-by-twelve of a wine bottle and glass, Peter's largest daily yet, appeared on his blog the next week. It was my turn to smile a Mona Lisa smile. Almost imperceptibly, except to his vigilant partner, he began to gravitate to eight-by-ten-inch and nine-by-twelve-inch paintings, and even dared an eleven-by-fourteen-inch, pulling canvases from the deep recesses of the studio.

"I want to add some variation to the size of my dailies," he explained, seemingly unconscious of any deeper significance, our earlier disagreement completely forgotten. "The larger canvas lets me add more to the composition."

It was just the kind of forward movement I had, drawing from all my years with him, anticipated he would be unable to resist. Despite his outward complacency, inside, Peter was just too dynamic a soul to rest on his laurels. It took real self-control, but I kept my lips zipped and let nature take its course. When he moved his studio from the main floor to the basement to give himself more space to step back and review larger work, I knew there would be no turning back.

Not surprisingly, the larger canvases took longer to paint. In this period of improving though still sluggish production, Peter was faced with a stylistic dilemma: whether to leave his strokes very loose to complete a piece in a single day or to finish with greater definition. Soft realism began taking the foreground over loose impressionism, and the bewitching van Gogh-ishness gradually faded into the shadows, emerging only on occasions when he needed to freshen his palette or get over a hump. There were van Gogh poinsettias, van Gogh baked bread and van Gogh's dog. Still, square inch by square inch, Peter was subtly acquiring a style while pushing the envelope from small to medium canvases entirely without my help. And I, though squirming and chafing under the self-imposed restraint, was learning the efficacy of a silent partnership.

Subject matter variation was part and parcel of the artist's size and style transition.

"Is that your reflection in the pocket watch?" I asked, looking so closely at his first trompe l'oeil (optical illusion), *Cowboy Dave,* that I got wet paint on my nose. The trompe l'oeil stood next to a triptych (three-sectioned painting) of garlic cloves and several large figuratives, worked from photo references, of the city flower market and park. There was also a series of profile portraits à la Andrew Wyeth along the wall. Both figuratives and profiles were a distinct departure from the earlier story portrait and still life work.

"You're trying to do an awful lot at once," I remarked. "New subject matter, speed, style and now a new genre. Plus your blog. Are you sure you're not over-extending or losing focus?"

"I have to keep moving," Peter insisted urgently. "I've come to the party late. I have to multi-task."

It was hard to argue his point. I could not help sharing his sense of panic when I reflected on how far I was from achieving anything meaningful from my own creative pursuits.

Even as his canvases took longer to complete, he continued his blog posts, sometimes just to lament his difficulties. The posts were a mix of honest self-critiques, progress paintings, and general art commentary sprinkled with self-deprecating humor that kept viewers coming back. "You lay yourself bare, don't you?" aptly commented one of his followers.

Peter also inserted occasional references to our evolving partnership in which my role now encompassed everything from cleaning the studio to emotional counseling. He'd started by simply calling me his "wife" (I'd asked not to be named), then had gradually transitioned into creative tags: Art Career Advisor, Art Consultant, Art Manager, Art Therapist, Business Manager, Chairwoman of the Official Registry of Painting Titles, Chief Title Officer CTO, Director of New Ideas, Director of Studio Morale, Houseplant Specialist, Inventory Manager, Official Chief Superintendent of Titles, Organizer, Painting Companion, Photographer, Productivity Moderator, Prop Master, Still Life Design Consultant, and Studio Decorator. He finally distilled my varied roles into the catch-all "She-

Who-Must-Not-Be-Named".

Readers enjoyed the labels and easily inferred from his posts that SWMNBN supervised his spending at antique stores, grew his props in the garden, steered the business side and generally kept him on the straight and narrow. More than any other part SWMNBN played, viewers recognized her contribution to Peter's painting titles. *Flower Study #2*, for example, was clearly not the work of SWMNBN. Visiting artists began posting confessions of their own titling struggles, and title job offers for SWMNBN started rolling in.

The SWMNBN appellation inferred a loftiness disproportionate to the simple jill-of-all-trades I had become. Chief Cook and Bottle Washer was closer to the truth. Still, it was the role of a lifetime, and I enjoyed the twists and turns of my digital personality each time I changed hats to meet the need of the moment. I never lost sight of the fact that SWMNBN was, after all, merely a reflective by-product of Peter's own nimble progression. Engineering to art. Portraits to still lifes. Still lifes to figuratives. Figuratives to Wyeth-esque portraits. Black rotary phone to blogger. Dailies to large canvases. Eclecticist to (almost) soft realist.

Tim Vine, the British comedian, is credited with this quote:
"So, I said to the gym instructor: 'Can you teach me to do the splits?'
He said: 'How flexible are you?'
I said: I can't make Tuesdays.'"

Peter was making it every day of the week, and I was tracking him closely to keep up. Agility was the constant in our partnership.

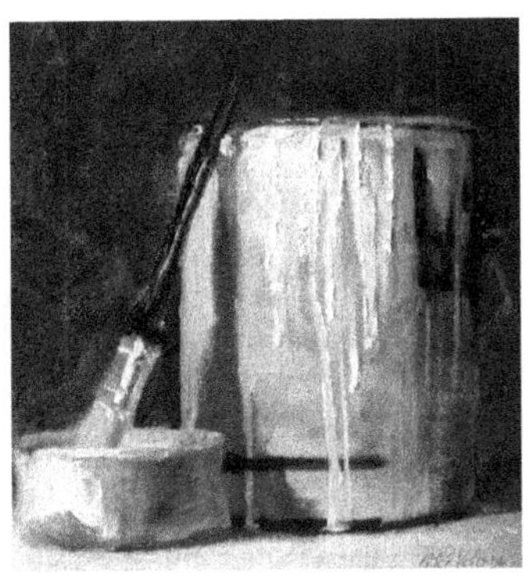

13

Suffusion

"Art is not a thing; it is a way."
—Elbert Hubbard

Since Peter had begun painting full-time, art was everywhere in our house—books, magazines, videos, still life set ups, drying paintings. There were stray paint spots on silverware, doorknobs, furniture, shoes and almost every piece of clothing he owned. Even his new studio companion, a Jack Russell and wire-haired terrier cross named Tasha (after Tasha Tudor, the illustrator and writer), occasionally sported paint in her hair.

I often felt overwhelmed, as if our lives had been colored over with a great tonal wash before I'd had a chance to reserve a clear corner for myself. I'm not sure what I'd expected. It wasn't this. I had my own job and I continued to follow my own interests in my spare time, but Peter's work dominated our home, and art had become our new lifestyle. I labored in the grey and analytical world of business management. He talked and worked and breathed art day and night. When I stepped over the threshold each evening, I felt like Dorothy when she emerged from the black and white house into the technicolor world of Oz.

One morning, I entered the kitchen to find Peter on the threshold of the basement stairs, coffee in hand, hair tousled, and still wearing his pajamas. One eyebrow raised, I scanned his appearance.

"Pajamas in the studio?" He looked down at his paint-stained flannels. "Not the first time, I see," I observed with meaning, making no attempt to hide my disapproval.

Paint on pajamas was just one step too far for me. It seemed reasonable, having surrendered the rest of the house, that when I slipped between the sheets, this should be a sacred, no-paint zone. Peter winced in acknowledgment, then started upstairs to change. I followed him.

There was something else nagging me about those pajamas. Years ago, when I'd left the office to work the family farm, I'd found the adjustment from starched suits to patched, stained farm clothes, however clean and comfortable, a real challenge. I'd insisted on ironing my shabby shirt and pants every day and starting out for the barn scrubbed and combed. It was a matter of personal dignity.

Peter was far less concerned with appearance; comfort was the sole determinant of what he wore each day. Yet, intuitively, I felt that the act of dressing for the studio was significant. It would put him in a better frame of mind to paint. It would make him take himself seriously.

"It seems to me that if you don't behave in all ways like you are a professional artist, you won't ever respect your own work."

I threw the matter at him with typical forthrightness, then left him with this food for thought, grabbing a paint-stained bath towel on my way out.

There is potency in small behaviors, but I sensed something even bigger lurking behind the pajama episode. Peter's new profession had quickly and completely suffused our home the way water color travels across absorptive paper. Though I felt inundated, he had, ironically, managed the kind of personal reserve that I craved. When pressed by our keen Council of Four on this point, he acknowledged the fact.

"I'm surrounded by art," he admitted, "I live and breathe it. But I don't know when I will actually feel the part of an artist."

"Is it because, once you commit to the part, the prospect of failure becomes more real?" I anticipated him.

"Yes," he hung his head.

"Are you an artist because you work as one or do you work as an artist because you are one?" Our daughter put the existential question only half facetiously.

"Either way," our son chimed in on a more serious note, "you will never *be* an artist unless you can *say* you are. You have to commit on the inside. Despite all this," he said, sweeping his arm to indicate the extent of our immersion, "I haven't yet heard you refer to yourself as an artist."

Peter fidgeted awkwardly but did not dismiss the wisdom. It's always a dose of cold water when you realize the students have become the teachers.

They continued their intervention.

"Let's hear you declare yourself!"

And, he did.

"*I* am an artist. I *am* an artist. I am an *artist*!"

I felt Peter's hard-won I-am-an-artist affirmation merited special recognition, so I surprised him one afternoon with a beautiful, blue leather La-Z-Boy recliner for the studio. He'd always wanted a recliner, and I rejoiced that his tastes were simple and manageable. We'd never have afforded a sports car. Though I intended the gift as a celebration of his commitment, my practicality inevitably crept in.

"You can use this chair to sit back comfortably from your work to evaluate it," I told him.

He nodded his acknowledgment and promptly took a nap in it. Then, he got paint on it. Finally, he began to use it as the comfy chair of judgment for which it was intended.

Unexpectedly, this gift doubled back on me. Peter's many studio hours and my job squeezed our precious little time together, and I found myself curling up in the recliner to be with him while he painted. If I could not carve out a paint-free space for myself in all this, I thought, I might as well make a place for myself right in the thick of it. "Ready for tea?" came my nightly invitation, and I carried two steaming, paint-smudged mugs to the basement with a book and a journal under my arm. The side-by-side part of the endeavor had become a very literal thing.

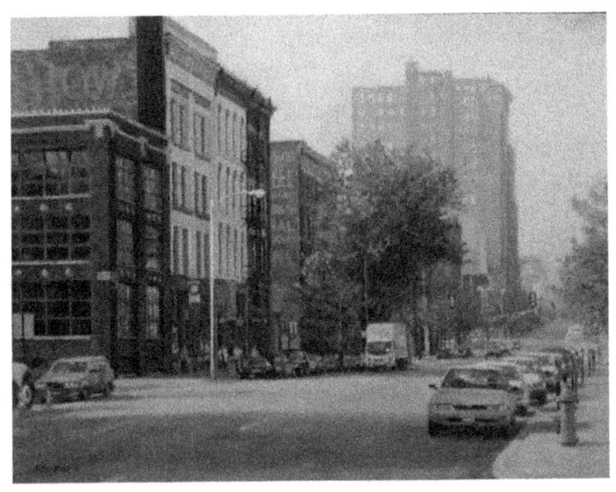

14

Art Marketing

"Realism has to be such high quality, you can't fake it.
It's all hanging out there like the laundry."
—Nelson Shanks

Two years had now passed since Peter quit engineering. By this time, ideas about his art career tumbled around in my mind like clothes in a dryer. From time to time, I needed to shake them out and either use them or put them away. On one particular occasion, I found myself unfolding a scheme of art marketing.

Though he'd produced an admirable volume of work, thus far, he had not done more than dabble with marketing. Aside from a rudimentary web site, a blog, a one-time ad in a national magazine and, later, eBay for the daily paintings, marketing had been a mere abstraction.

Neither of us had yet broached the topic seriously, though for distinctly different reasons: I had judged it too soon in Peter's development for a formal marketing strategy, and Peter had always assumed that paintings done well would eventually just…sell. I doubted he was the only new artist heavy on paint and light on salesmanship. Anyway, so much about his work and intentions had changed since he'd first put paint to canvas that we would have scrapped any earlier plans.

"Can we talk?" I asked one morning.

"Uh-oh," came his reply.

That we headed for the living room couch was an indication of the importance of our meeting. A full-blown strategy session merited the couch, the board room of our home, where the big stuff got decided. Peter poured the coffee, and I sat, afghan across my legs against the air conditioning, with pen and notebook in hand ready to record our combined brilliance.

"The internet has given you a great start on exposure and name recognition," I began. "What are your other options?"

I expected Peter to amaze me by spilling out all the marketing research he'd quietly done while I was at work but had never mentioned. I was not disappointed. He grabbed a pile of art business books and magazines off the bookshelf.

"There are a bunch of art consultants," he began, spreading them in front of me. "It seems to me that they are valuable less for finding sales venues than for keeping the artist on track from a business standpoint. I already have a partner who does that."

He stopped and smiled appreciatively at me. Suddenly, he was rattling off avenues of every kind—associations, art shows, art fairs, galleries, home shows, advertising and so on—down which he could peddle his work. As we sorted through these outlets, I looked longingly out the window at the sunny day we were missing while we labored indoors.

"How about that art fair in Des Moines this weekend?" I asked, throwing the afghan aside and shifting over to the desk to browse for details. "Let's just go! We'll do some reconnaissance first hand. Action usually spurs genius, and even if it doesn't, we'll at least have seen some art and enjoyed this day."

Within hours, we were strolling around the fair checking out art booths. The artists were generous with their time and information about costs, rates of sales, everything we asked.

"I can't say I like the way the art is exposed to the elements—sun, wind, rain—in those open tents. That can't be good for the work," Peter said quietly as we took a hummus and pita break. "And I don't see much realism. Mostly design-ish work."

A well-dressed young couple dropped into the seats next to us and struck up a conversation over their sandwiches and coffee. They were collectors, they announced. They had so much art, bragged the man, that when they'd relocated for a new job, it had cost over $15,000 just to ship it! He had gotten his new employer to pick up the bill, he told us, laughing heartily. They hopped up to go buy more artwork, and Peter handed each of them one of his new business cards.

As they left, he turned to me with a thoughtful frown.

"I don't think they collect realism if they're excited about this show." He signaled in the direction of the tents, then paused. "I wonder if this fair is representative of the overall circuit."

We didn't concern ourselves with the answer once we learned the extent to which fair exhibitors were away from home. Their lifestyle was more suited to RV living.

"That's not for us," Peter declared.

"You've come a long way if you can let go of your romantic image of life on the road in an art Winnebago," I teased on the drive home, scratching art fairs from consideration in my notebook. "Not bad for one day's work."

The freak storm with winds over one hundred miles per hour that would blow through Omaha's own annual art fair that season would only reinforce this decision.

"The obvious next step is brick-and-mortar galleries," Peter ventured. I shifted my position in the seat to listen.

Galleries were a puzzle to me, a kind of mystery zone. We had a lot of anecdotal information from fellow artists, but there was really no single comprehensive source from which we could learn about them. Each gallery, like each artist, seemed to have a personality of its own.

"I'll just have to knock on doors and search web sites to acquaint myself with them one by one," he concluded resignedly.

And he did. Introverted as ever, his audacity astounded me. He just walked into area galleries unannounced. With business cards in hand, and a web site to view, he could very quickly introduce his work to the gallery owner and receive a thumbs up or thumbs down on the spot. The method was hard on the soul but saved time in the long run, and it conditioned the stomach, both Peter's and mine. I made sure to stock up on Cheerios.

Peter's first success with the pound-the-pavement approach was a small area gallery. The owner seemed interested in the variety his paintings would add to her collection. She stuck to small canvases, which suited Peter, who hadn't yet built a store of finished larger work. It did not escape him that the other work in the gallery was entirely design-ish and abstract.

"I'll be the contrast," he reasoned optimistically. "Better to have things on public display than sitting in my studio."

He had a point. And a humble beginning is still a beginning.

Shortly after, the owner approached him, asking, "Do you have any city-scapes, especially big ones?"

Peter had none but took the hint and dashed off to paint some urban scenes. City life was not a natural fit for this tree-hugging, nature-loving man, so he had to work extremely hard to find inspiration as well as the courage and tenacity to finish work outside his comfort zone. When he returned to the gallery with a few hard-won street scenes, each twenty-four by thirty inches, the owner shook her head. "I really don't have room for those." His mouth dropped open, then closed again. He picked up the pieces and walked out.

"Why would she do that?" he asked in frustration that evening.

I was uncertain how to reply, but the message that emerged from this episode was clear and powerful.

"Maybe the paintings are bigger than she expected. Or maybe it was just a brainchild of the moment." I paused thoughtfully. "You'll always want to please galleries but you'll have to be careful not to chase random requests that take you off the path. Set your own boundaries. Move toward what you do best."

He nodded as I scratched this lesson into my journal.

The search for urban landscapes brought Peter to Lincoln, Nebraska, a mere 45-minute drive from home. Lincoln is a small university town, where he hoped to discover scenes appealing to

Midwest collectors. True to his commitment, he knocked on the door of every gallery in town while he was there. The most promising was owned by a small, energetic woman. Her taste was fine, and her gallery a well displayed mixture of styles and media. She and Peter connected instantly. Before he knew it, his work was on her gallery walls, and she was offering him a show.

Peter's excitement was infectious as he lined up his works-in-progress for the show along the studio wall and asked for my critique.

"I don't really know what I'm talking about," I resisted uncomfortably, not wanting to steer him the wrong way. I'd learned so much, but that didn't mean my opinion and that of the buying public were anything alike.

"Yes, you do. You already know more than you think. And anyway, what I really need is your first impression when you look at the paintings. Tell me what stands out to you."

That, I thought, I could handle. Mine was a practical critique with a narrow focus, but he seemed satisfied, and I loved him all the more for the trust he'd placed in me.

I created a postcard announcement for the show and handed it out left and right to all my business contacts, which inevitably prompted discussions about art in general.

"My friend just paid $10,000 each for two paintings," recounted an associate. "Two square white canvases, each with a single, large arrow on it. I'm not sure how they're to be hung," she giggled. "I can't figure out which way the arrows are supposed to point."

I took this story home to Peter, and we laughed until our sides ached. I felt I could excuse our little joke at the expense of abstract and design artists since they were the ones laughing all the way to the bank. In all seriousness, abstract and design prices as compared to realism were truly a mystery to us both when we considered the skill and labor that went into the latter.

The following spring, Peter found two well-established galleries to take his work.

"What a gift," he exclaimed. "These galleries are proven over time and represent artists in all styles!"

One gallery manager had examined his paintings down to the brush stroke. Peter had returned impressed, gratified to be chosen, and hopeful about this representation.

"Four gallery representations in a single year!"

I burst with vicarious pride and excitement. Taking marketing from an abstraction to a working reality was proving to be an art unto itself, involving both our heads, not just one.

"I think we can safely declare that you have graduated from professional art school and are entering the *professional* stage," I said, inaugurating the next five-year plan.

I turned to a fresh page.

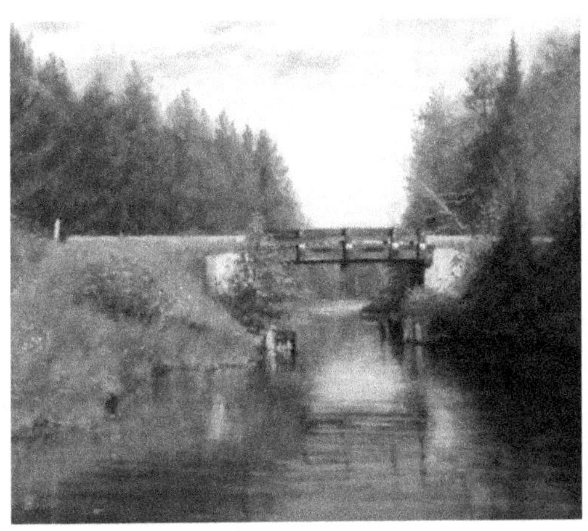

15

Artistic Paralysis

"Painting is easy when you don't know how, but very difficult when you do."
—Edgar Degas

With only a handful of exceptions, the works accepted by the galleries were still life and figurative paintings. Peter had not yet embraced landscapes, and the few outdoor scenes he'd painted were done in the studio from photo references. The plein air painting resurgence burgeoning across the country had not yet captivated him. Quite the contrary, plein air painting continued to be a trial.

On his first serious attempt beyond little color sketches of our neighborhood, he chose a very secluded spot so he could paint without spectators. After setting up at the end of a long and solitary riverside road, he looked up to spy a police car slowly making its way down the road toward the easel.

"What are you doing?" the cop asked when he stepped from the vehicle.

Peter stared at the man and answered hesitatingly, as if this were a trick question, "I'm painting."

He threw a look toward the easel, brushes and paint that were a dead giveaway. Then, just to be sure, he handed the man his business card and studied his reaction. The officer checked both sides as if the card might be fraudulent, then returned it.

"OK, but don't go anywhere up the banks. That's private property."

Peter looked up at the opulent houses that lined the riverfront and understood.

"It's like that privileged neighborhood had its own dedicated police force," he told me and the Council of Four on Skype. "I guess the terror alert was cadmium orange today," he added, making light of the incident as he held up a small study of the Platte River for review.

This was a delightful anecdote for my collection, but experiences like the riverfront did nothing to quell Peter's discomfort painting in public. And mild agoraphobia wasn't the artist's only problem. With his slow speed, he could not keep up with the shifting light and, after chasing it, ended with a work that was washed out and lacking in contrasts.

"I'm just not a natural plein air painter," he moaned.

Despite all this, or perhaps because of it, he felt it was time to tackle the landscape demon head on. He found a plein air painting workshop hosted by Deb Groesser, a nationally recognized Omaha painter whose ease, graciousness and sheer joy in her work were food for his soul.

"She used my painting to point out to the class what *not* to do," he chuckled when he got home. "That's exactly the kind of lesson I need."

He'd been hungering for frank and meaningful instruction and had returned home invigorated and anxious to quickly implement all he had learned.

The first positive step had to do with equipment.

"I have to get rid of this," he said, unloading the stylish French plein air easel he'd bought especially for the class and unceremoniously shoving it into a studio corner. "The instructor had a Pochade box on a tripod for quicker set up. I liked it much better."

He took an old wooden paint box, cut out the middle section

and reconnected the outer pieces, then stuck this atop an old camera tripod.

"What is that?" I asked, looking at the hideous contraption held together with an extraordinary amount of duct tape and casting a pained sideways glance at the already retired French easel.

"It's my new pochade box," he announced so proudly I repressed the emerging lecture on waste from my inner accountant. Intrigued at this sudden and serious turn, I put on my spectator hat and waited to see where it would take him.

Peter began a painfully slow program to overcome his plein air avoidance, beginning with rural Midwest landscapes. Day after day, he traipsed all over the countryside surrounding Omaha and Lincoln in search of subject matter.

"I'm just not drawn to the scenery out here," he sighed again and again after each jaunt. "The sky is magnificent but dominates the scene, and I want to paint more than sky."

I suspected that what he really wanted in his heart was in short supply in Nebraska: water and trees. You could take the boy out of the East Coast, but you couldn't shake the East Coast out of the boy.

In time, these plein air trips came to a complete standstill. Scrutinizing the artist, it became clear to me that something larger than unimpressive scenery was hindering his progress. This was not a grain-of-sand-in-your-shoe type impediment, it turned out; it was a rock formation. Despite his professed determination, Peter had developed a blockage, a complete and total wall, to plein air painting. Literally, he could not touch the brush to the canvas, as though an invisible force was holding back his hand. He would stand in front of the easel, wet brush tip wavering inches from the surface struggling to make a single stroke. It was ten times worse if anyone was standing nearby.

"What is going on?" I'd ask over and over again.

He'd just shake his head, unable to articulate it.

That his paralysis was related to outdoor painting was ironic, in light of his love of nature, but clear, as he continued his studio still lifes unabated. I made attempts to chip away at the problem, parroting back to Peter many of the things he'd said to me.

"It's only a study," I'd remind him.

"Just try to get the values down."

"Take a break."

Or, "Just record the key colors."

And, "Oils are very forgiving."

The student had become the teacher, though to no avail, because the teacher was making no inroads. I even engaged the Council of Four to help pull him from this quagmire. Their efforts were no more effective than mine. What was needed to break through this wall was not chipping but wielding a pickaxe. It was the tough love role I detested but was so good at, or so Peter always told me. And it was exhausting for us both. Peter tolerated my incessant interrogating and pounding because he intuitively understood that, left alone, he'd remain at an indefinite impasse.

He was seriously stuck, and his usual ways of getting unstuck, talking it through with me or spending time outside, were not working. Only once before, when he was working long hours under an unrelenting boss, had I watched helplessly as he'd sunk into a funk this deep that overspread us like a thick fog. It had taken an illness to break him out back then. The present funk was insidiously spreading, sapping his enthusiasm and infecting our partnership and our marriage with an impenetrable barrier to communication. Fear took hold of me, and a knot of panic settled into my gut.

Due either to uncanny timing or spectacular telepathy, some dear friends invited us, at the peak of Peter's crisis, to visit their cabin in the North Woods of Wisconsin, encouraging him to paint as much as he liked. This was our first invitation to the home of a couple we'd cherished instantly upon first meeting, so it was a meaningful trip for Peter and me and one we anticipated with great pleasure. With mixed emotions, I watched as the artist, in the full grip of dysfunction, mechanically added the last of his supplies to the hatchback. Heavy in spirit, we headed north.

The very best of hosts, our friends planned to hike and boat us to places of the utmost beauty, always stopping for breathtaking views and painting attempts.

"What are you doing?" asked one of them mid-trail in the shade of a scrumptious pine forest. Peter and I had stopped, eyes closed, wind picking up our hair.

"Listening to the symphony of the trees," I said ecstatically.

Oh, how we'd missed this sound! Hearing it was like relieving a great muscle ache you didn't know you had. It opened my eyes more fully to Peter's big sky landscape dilemma, but the antidote to the plein air blockage still eluded us both.

One perfect Wisconsin day, we anchored in a narrow strip of water in front of an old bridge trellis to allow Peter to paint from the boat. He began the process of setting up while, in characteristic style, our ever-prepared friends pulled out drinks and snacks to relax in the moment. I turned around after accepting a glass to find the artist standing as still as a statue, brush frozen about two inches from the canvas. I charged in like a drill sergeant.

"Just paint! Put something on that canvas…anything!"

My face was heated pink with the consciousness that our friends had stepped back as far as the little boat would allow, clearly appalled yet giving us the space we so obviously needed. There was no time to give a proper explanation. Even if I'd had time, what would I have said? I had no name for this phenomenon but I knew with absolute certainty that if Peter just managed to make contact with the canvas, the spell would be broken. My assault did not stop until the brush landed. Just 20 minutes from that first stroke, he finished a study out of which arose one of his loveliest plein air landscapes, like a phoenix out of ashes: *Where Still Waters Lead.*

Back at home, Peter held up the final canvas. The light was back in his eyes, and he was thanking me for my tenacity. He had painted three stunning Wisconsin plein air landscapes from that trip, all of which are among his best work to date. I looked up from writing to admire the work and breathed a heavy sigh, relieved this burden was past and thankful our partnership had not become a casualty in the battle for Peter's plein air psyche.

Years passed before we fully understood the Great Paralysis of Peter's art career. Next to the accomplished work in his studio, he had been mortified at his amateurish landscapes, seized with a complete loss of confidence and had locked up, plain and simple. The mental picture and the rendering were incongruent, and the imperfect practice too unworthy to persist. This all happened in an irrational blink of an eye, of course, which made the story so much harder to intellectually unravel. Although he's had many occasions since when he's gotten stuck, none so overpowering ever happened again.

We owe a lot to the friends who encouraged Peter, who withheld judgment on that fateful day on the boat and who ignited our love for the North Woods. The waters calmed us. The blowing trees soothed our city-worn souls. The fresh, pine-scented air was a tonic. We sucked it through our nostrils as though we'd never breathe again, clearing away the dust of the Plains. The forests were invigorating to the point of putting a bounce in our steps, and we can still recall the hollow thud of our footsteps as we treaded over great networks of old tree roots. Most importantly, we could sense the tremendous life force in those forests. *Eureka!* This is what was missing in the Plains. One visit to Wisconsin—and a great deal of forbearance by our friends— was all it took for the artist to regain his traction.

And, on top of all this, our friends invited us back the next year.

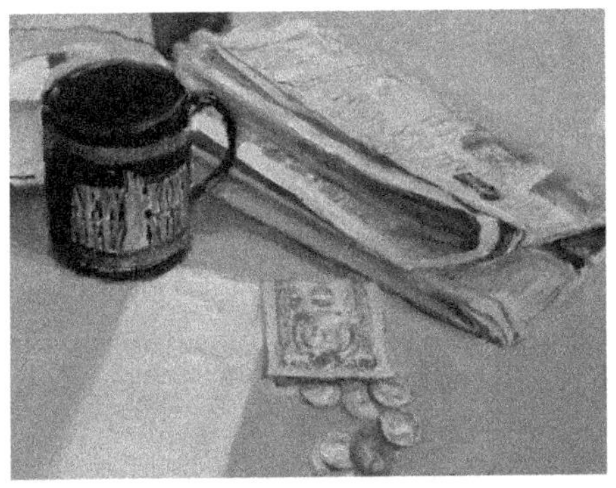

16

New Palette

"Every new beginning comes from some other beginning's end."
—Seneca

Just two years into his daily paintings, Peter surprised me by abruptly announcing his intention to abandon them altogether.

"I've lost touch with the soul of my painting," he confessed. "I need a new path."

Without knowing where he would go next, he stopped cold and withdrew from the Daily Painters Guild. It pained him to see his blog following dwindle for shortage of posts, but he claimed to need all his focus to sort himself out. I sensed serious change in the offing but was so preoccupied at the office that I had little energy to delve into this dilemma.

"What would van Gogh do?" I teased, trying to keep the mood light.

"I don't know," came his unexpectedly sober response. "I have to do something different. I'm getting stale."

To shake loose, he started attending a series of life drawing sessions, taught a few art classes and planned pieces for upcoming exhibitions. More than once, uncertainty and slow production rekindled the lure of the daily-painting days. Speed of painting continued to be his particular bedevilment. No matter how much it improved, it was never enough.

"It's so hard to walk away from something that worked," he vacillated for the umpteenth time. "If only I could produce large work more quickly and consistently."

"You will," I assured him. "The attraction of the small paintings is the turnaround time, feeling like you've accomplished something." He waited expectantly. "OK, it's the regular cash, too," I conceded, "but even the small canvases are taking you longer to achieve than before now that your style has tightened up a bit. You'll get faster in time."

The owner of a small gallery had called some time ago to say she no longer wanted to sell fine art. Peter had retrieved his few remaining pieces from her walls and persisted largely unfazed. Things were otherwise looking good from his studio chair. His paintings were moving in the other galleries. Several still lifes and his first landscape entry were accepted into national art association shows. His trompe l'oeil *Cowboy Dave* was awarded the American Plains Artists Award of Excellence. He'd closed the year with respectable financial success. We had every reason to hope.

To our surprise, the Lincoln gallery, which had sold prolifically for Peter, abruptly closed, leaving him with just two remaining galleries. Over the next few months, the larger of the two began calling. "Can you discount this painting?" The piece had been hanging for a while, so Peter agreed. "The customer doesn't like the frame. Can you give us another one?" He did. "Can you paint something about Omaha?" He did. The telling remark finally came: "Your prices are too high."

"If I make my prices any lower," Peter complained miserably, "I'll have to pay the gallery to take them."

Without a word, the larger gallery closed just nine months after Peter had penned his name on the contract, and he found himself knocking on the door to retrieve his work. With only one gallery representation remaining, he sought the comfort of the familiar and checked his former daily painting outlet.

"eBay sales for daily painters have dropped," he reported, puzzled.

The final blow came when an artist friend dropped in unannounced at the last gallery to see Peter's work on display. There was none. The gallery manager, Peter discovered, had moved all Peter's pieces to a back closet without a word. Once about 80% realism, the walls were now entirely covered with abstract and design work. Peter could not hide his exasperation as we loaded his canvases into the car.

"They could have called me to pick these up rather than just store them without notice," he grumbled.

Later in the car, he reasoned more soberly, "With all the galleries closing, I guess I can't blame them for shifting to abstract, if that's all that's selling." I could not match his magnanimity in that moment. "Gallery owners have to eat, too," he looked over at me with a different kind of realism.

By the spring of 2008, Peter had been represented by four galleries. By June, 2009, all his work was back in the studio.

"What's going on?" he asked despairingly, head in his hands.

What was going on? Among other things, *The Great Recession*. In answer to our desperate bargain for change, opportunity had steered us away from the vulnerable East Coast, just as the financial crisis had been insidiously, and to our ignorance, building its momentum there.

During our search for a place to live in Omaha, the largest cyclone we'd ever seen had hovered threateningly overhead, and sirens sounded all over the city, forcing us to take refuge in the mall. Great swirling storms were part of Omaha life, and Omahans took them in stride. The financial storm was a force of a different nature, and I felt all the good fortune of our predicament in spite of its impact on art. The downturn did not spare the Midwest, though it struck with somewhat milder force than on the coasts. Sure, we felt the September 29 stock crash and saw downsizing, closures, depressed housing and tightened belts, but unemployment remained mercifully low.

Despite the dire predictions for the industry, my workplace, a professional services firm, had as productive a year as ever.

"I know it's been hard on your art, but this is exactly how a partnership is meant to work," I spoke consolingly to Peter. "When one of us is down, the other is there for support. Fortunately, my job has not been affected. How can we feel anything except gratitude right now?" I asked earnestly as we looked to the future with an optimism most Americans could not share.

My own optimism, I had to admit, was not absolute. The downturn that wiped out Peter's earnings also bound me to the office more tightly and indefinitely than I'd ever been. Deep inside, a part of me felt stifled, as though it was locked in a dark room without a window. I held fast to my bargain with Peter but took refuge in the only place I could, redoubling my writing.

The financial crisis, it turned out, was not the only force depressing Peter's sales. He and I had erred in our calculations, misinterpreting the conservative predisposition of the Midwest to mean that Midwesterners would prefer representational art. How wrong we had been. Most area galleries dealt in abstract and design work, and the few who had represented realists had now closed.

"Our clients don't really like realism," one defunct gallery had argued as a reason to lower prices.

Peter hadn't bought the argument.

"Something's not right," he asserted as we reconvened on the boardroom couch with tea and popcorn. "And it's not my prices. They're already low. We were wrong about the Midwest. Money is not the issue. Abstract and design work sells at any price. No, this is about style. I have to find my way into other markets that favor realism."

I sat back to take in and record the wisdom of his words. The art galleries, the bedrock of our marketing strategy, were gone. We scraped off the whole palette and started again with a clean brush.

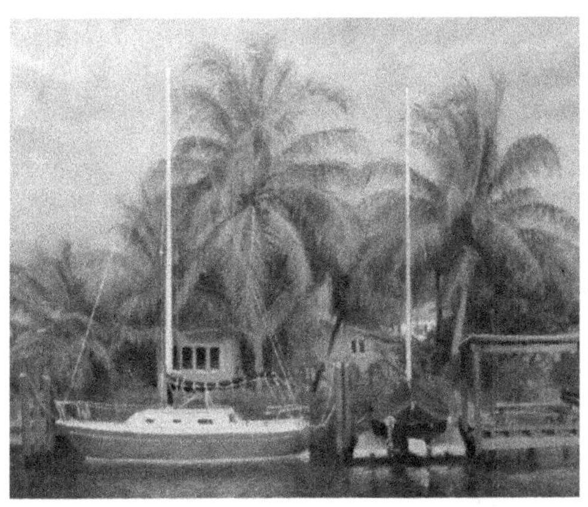

17

Competition

"My greatest competition is, well, me."
—R. Kelly

Peter persisted in his pursuit of gallery representation despite the economic climate. Thanks to our trips to the Wisconsin Northwoods, he put together a series of paintings and began systematically searching for galleries in the state of Wisconsin.

"They won't take my paintings," he turned to me in consternation after hanging up the phone with the third Wisconsin gallery, "because I have no connection to the state."

I shook my head in disbelief.

"These are great paintings." I scanned his beautiful and growing collection sitting idly in the studio with no hope of an outlet. "Art has so many unwritten rules, it's a wonder anyone paints," I reflected sympathetically. "Now what?" I asked him pointedly, having no suggestion of my own. "We have to find your market."

He nodded thoughtfully. I could see from his eyes that the man was down but not out.

At the same time, he continued his pursuit of juried memberships in reputed art associations and was accepted into the International Guild of Realism (IGOR) based on his still life work.

"Wow," I responded to this latest notice. "If you needed confirmation of how far you've come, there it is."

"Yeah," he agreed, adding in characteristic humility, "but looking at the other members' work, all I see is that I have a long way to go."

More than anything, I admired the way he was always reaching.

He received word that his *Carafe sur Rouge* still life was accepted into IGOR's show in Naples, Florida.

"Wanna go?" he asked.

I stared at him.

"Sunshine in February? Getting away with you? Is this a trick question?" I asked, running to the closet to see if I had any beach wear that would still fit.

In the recesses of my wardrobe, my enthusiasm melted into panic. I was not very good at these affairs. I loved meeting new people, but these would be art connections important to Peter's career, and (cringe) I'd have to remember their names. I could recall conversations and phone numbers. I could quote movies and financial statements but inevitably struggled to fill in the blank after I said "Hello". I voiced my worries to Peter, and we both laughed nervously.

"You know I'll be of no help," he confessed. "I'm worse than you are at it."

I hoped Naples had patience for the socially handicapped.

Mensch that he was, Peter didn't have a competitive cell in his body. High school wrestling aside, I've never met a person so entirely dispassionate about winning. He definitely wanted success, though for Peter, this meant selling his work at reasonable prices and becoming an accepted realist among his peers.

"There's plenty of room for us all," he maintained. "We don't have to be pitted against one another."

With this mindset, the pressure was off, and we traveled south unconcerned about awards and ribbons and ready to enjoy this memorable milestone in his career.

After curling our blue Nebraskan toes in the toasty Florida

sand, we headed for the artists' reception in sunny Naples. Carefully observing Peter's rules of etiquette, we quietly moved from one painting to the next, taking each in and identifying serious talent in the room. Peter was a painting or two ahead of me, and I arrived in front of a still life of a clock and old books to find him and the artist, Bob, already in comfortable conversation.

I was introduced to Bob and then to his wife, Paulette. I instinctively loved this woman, and she instantly put me at ease with a candid recital of her challenges and love supporting her husband's art ambitions. I threw my head back in a loud shriek of laughter that drew Peter's and Bob's smiling attention and startled looks from everyone else in the vicinity. Paulette had just delivered the punch line of a classic moment in a close art partnership when Bob was sure he had finished a piece but she, the partner, knew better.

"He signed it with such a flourish, you know, and then I said, so you think you're finished, do you?"

Meeting Bob and Paulette was one of those magical moments, like when an artist realizes that her painting has transformed into something deliciously greater than the sum of the strokes. Talking with them was absolutely effortless, and all our worries about social unfitness melted away. New art friends. What an unexpected find. We sat with them at dinner and learned they were a few years older and both recently retired, so Bob, like Peter, was new to professional art and starting a second career. Paulette was not the financial backer but she filled so many of the same roles as I that we connected on multiple levels. The talk and laughter continued unabated through dessert and coffee.

The evening came to an end all too soon, and we were all leaving for home the next day. Bob and Paulette kindly dropped us off at our hotel after dinner. As we climbed the stairs to our room, I could see Peter was as thrilled by this new friendship as I.

"I can't believe we found friends like this!" I said excitedly. "They get it, the partnership part. No explanations necessary. As soon as we get home, we have to call them and figure out how to get together again."

I was reminded of Jane Austen's character, Marianne, in *Sense and Sensibility*, who, when chided by her sister Elinor for not being more reserved in new company, replied: "It is not time or opportunity that is to determine intimacy: it is disposition alone. Seven years would be insufficient to make some people acquainted with each other, and seven days are more than enough for others."

Or seven minutes with Bob and Paulette.

Peter and I flew home so much richer than when we had departed. We had the experience of an international exhibition under our belts and new feedback on his work. We had the warmth of Florida sunshine in our bones and the promise of new friendship, the kind that is more like the reconvening of old souls.

All too soon, we returned to work, and I was trudging in on Monday night out of a heavy snow, looking forward to a hot, home-cooked meal.

Peter met me at the door.

"What is it?" I asked, frowning at his grave face.

"Bob and Paulette never made it home. They were killed by a drunk driver on the way to the Miami airport. I think we were the last to see them," he blurted out in a single stream of breath.

I stood absolutely motionless, Paulette's lilted voice and infectious laughter from just forty-eight hours ago still ringing in my ears.

For many weeks, Peter and I alternated between numbness and grief. We mourned this close couple and the comfortable retirement and art career they would never experience. We felt pain for their family left to deal with their premature and unjust end. We grieved the loss of a friendship forged in one evening yet deeper than many we'd had for years.

Bob and Paulette had transformed us in a single evening, and we thanked them.

In fond memory of Bob and Paulette

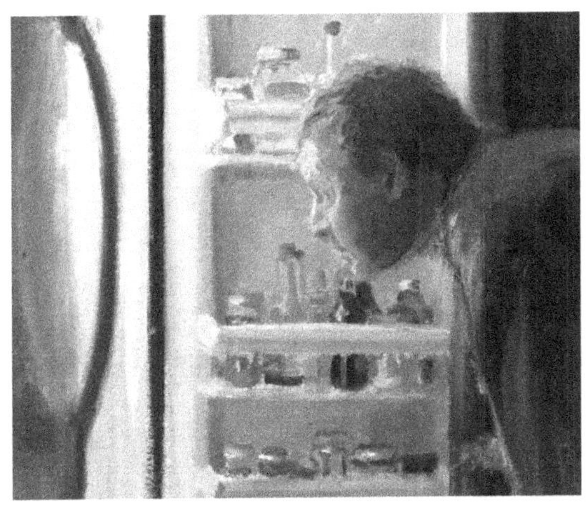

18

Art Psychology

"The soul becomes dyed with the color of its thoughts."
— Marcus Aurelius

From the very start of his art endeavor, Peter had felt a heightened vulnerability and pressure having begun so late in life. Once begun, he'd experienced waves of change, recurring uncertainty, creative paralysis, the economic downturn and, most recently, the passing of friends. Pushing hard to get ahead, he'd walked away from the daily painting rush that had fed his soul for so long. The result, at least for a time, was a quiet and sluggish artist.

"Do you choose your palette according to your mood?" I asked him one evening from the recliner.

I had just taken a webinar about the use of color in advertising and its effects on consumers' emotions, which had set me wondering. Is the opposite true? Does the artist subconsciously select his palette based on his feelings of the moment? It seemed to me to be a very pertinent topic in the face of Peter's deflated mood. He stared down at his brush thoughtfully pondering my question.

The psychology of everything fascinated me and, in the course of my partnership with Peter, I naturally gravitated to the psychology of the artist. He was the handy and captive subject for my little research project. I observed him keenly and was interested in what made him tick normally on one day and dysrhythmically the next. It was impossible to be entirely objective, but I did try to take clear stock of the person. He was smart, highly imaginative and deeply feeling. He was generally happy and optimistic but prone to occasional down periods which snuffed out his creative angel. He had no idea what triggered the downslides. Was it his Slavic heritage, last night's dinner, too many paint fumes, or sleep deprivation? My hypothesis: Helping my partner understand and manage his mood fluctuations would help his painting.

We expect artists to feel deeply because, we contend, feelings are the wellspring of their creations. We accept the purported link between creativity and mood, maintaining that genius arises from and even pre-requires some degree of despondency. In exchange for their suffering, we give artists tremendous latitude of temperament and extend similar license to attire, behavioral eccentricities and even hygiene. This expectation condemns the artist to an incessant ebbing and flowing between heightened creativity and *melancholia,* a lovely old word for a devil of a thing. Was this the destiny of every artist, being a social oddity on a predetermined roller coaster ride? I did not want to see my partner in life and in art, or any other artist, for that matter, caught endlessly in this up and down cycle.

"I can be depressed painting yellow and thrilled painting gray," Peter finally answered. "Mood influences which painting I paint and whether or not I pick up a particular challenge but not the choice of colors on my palette. Those are pretty much set."

It was my turn to be thoughtful for a few minutes.

"So," I resumed the thread, "how can you be sure you keep your mood out of it?" I lifted the book off my lap and turned a photo of Jackson Pollock's *Blind Spot* toward him, a depressing canvas of black and brown spots that would drown the spirit of anyone in the room. "There are some things an artist should just keep to himself," I said, making a face.

He laughed.

"For me, as a realist, painting isn't about how I feel that day," he answered. "It's transferring what I see—beauty in patterns of lights and darks, warms and cools—to the canvas. I look at a painting over a period of time so no single day or mood can take it over."

Was it really that simple? Mood affected the clothes I wore, the food I ate, the books I read, and the company I kept. Many days, it took a serious act of will to override my prevailing mood. I tucked the question away for further study.

To pull himself up and out of his torpor, Peter took on a challenge: painting self-portraits, one portrait each day for thirty days. Whenever he challenged himself, he got the best results by committing publicly on his blog so others could help him see it through if he began to waver. I watched as the portraits accumulated, each revealing a different face of the same person to the world. If ever the art psychologist wanted validation of an artist's inner fluctuations, here was the evidence.

Collectively, however, the portraits proved the efficacy of his own mood-leavening antidote: deadlines. "I forget I'm down when I have to work to a deadline," he declared energetically as he sat before his mirror, brush furiously working self-portrait number 22. "I get really focused." (The art psychologist dutifully made a note of this in the file.)

The portrait series ended in a wonderfully upbeat sketch of Peter sitting in front of his easel surrounded by Rembrandt, Rockwell, Homer and Whistler, entitled *Heroes*.

It wasn't easy to sustain the pitch and clarity of the challenge when he returned to routine work. Not long after the 30th portrait, I poked my head into the studio on my way back out to the garden and observed, "You don't seem to be making much headway on that one. You're working the same spot you were working when I first went out this morning."

I often cringed at my own candor, but Peter insisted on it, as I insisted on his. Our long history together made it possible for each of us to accept hard truths from each other. His brush continued its almost frantic motion on the canvas, and I could sense that he was tight with compulsivity and frustration. Anxiety had kicked in. Or a creative block. Which came first? From where I sat as resident art psychologist, this was the chicken-and-egg question for artists. Here was Peter, caught in a loop, painting without progressing like a record needle stuck in a scratch on an old 33 RPM album.

Overpainting, he had taught me, was a danger sign. He had trained his personal counselor what to say when she found him like this. I stepped up to the easel.

"Put the painting away," I said dutifully, but gently. He gave me a deer-in-the-headlights look, which told me I'd picked the right intervention. "Put it away for a while," I repeated. "Let's go out in the garden."

That last part was my own idea.

He stepped outside first, and I discreetly reached over and pulled a dirty paint brush out of his tea cup before joining him.

"Thanks for the rescue," he said sincerely as we slowly walked the tomato row. Then, he added, "You know, I have your voice in my head."

"Oh, God, that must be awful," I winced.

"No, it's actually a good thing," he assured me. "When I get stuck, I ask myself what you would say, and I hear your answer. It helps me out."

"Funny, but I do the same with you." I echoed the sentiment, smiling.

He took my hand, and we continued our leisurely garden stroll, popping juicy cherry tomatoes into our mouths from the overloaded vines. As complicated as moods can be, give the artist a fresh cherry tomato, and all is right with the world. Sometimes, all the psychology you need is in your own backyard.

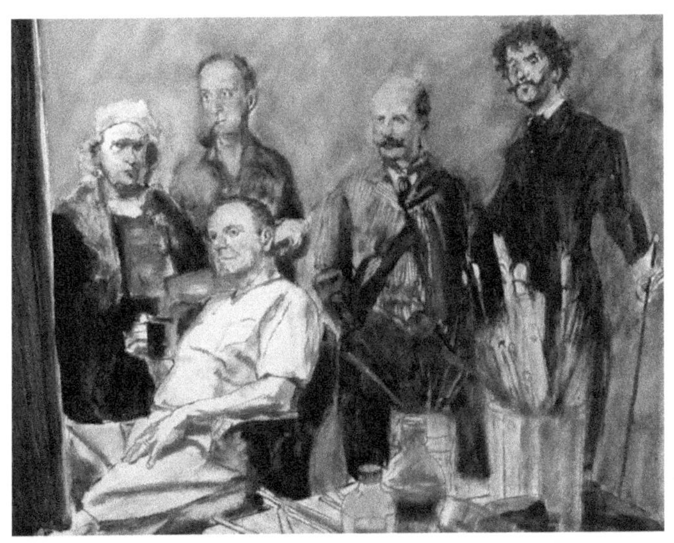

Heroes, oil sketch, Peter Yesis

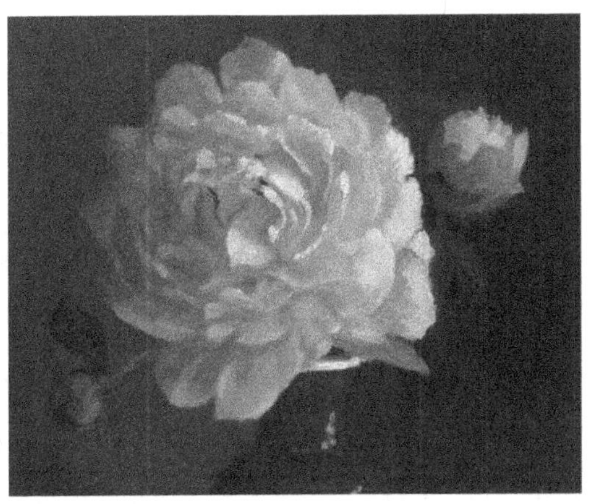

19

The Sweet Spot

"Be sure you put your feet in the right place, then stand firm."
—Abraham Lincoln

Looking back, 2009 was a pivotal year, not that we were keen to it at the time. The loss of all the Midwest galleries was offset by a single success that would wholly redirect Peter's energy.

"I just got accepted into a New Jersey gallery!" he told me excitedly on the phone.

He couldn't hold onto this news until I got home from work, and I was glad to share his excitement in real time. Having both been born and raised in New Jersey, there was a certain "Welcome home" quality to this representation.

"I'd love to think it was due to my work alone," he added wishfully. "I'm sure my connection to the state added value."

He'd found the gallery on the internet and had sent an email request for consideration along with a link to his web site, which was now populated with a fair volume of paintings. Lise, the owner, had called to express her delight with his work and to request some paintings. Belying the twelve-hundred-mile gap between Nebraska and New Jersey, the introduction was virtually immediate, a far cry from only a few years earlier when galleries still required snail mail submissions of expensive slides or CDs.

"There are some holdouts for the traditional method," Peter told me, "but I don't think they'll hang onto the old ways for long."

The internet really was an amazingly transformative vehicle, and the art world was a beneficiary of it.

Technology was not the only thing that was different in that year. The subprime crisis had rolled over us all, leaving massive unemployment in its wake. In the ensuing recession, the whole economy had the jitters. Many were down and out, well-established artists and galleries among them.

"I have a lot more candidates for job openings," I reflected aloud over dinner, "and Nebraska isn't anywhere near as depressed as the coasts. I cringe imagining what it's like out there."

"I see it in my searches," Peter reported dejectedly. "I'm finding fewer galleries, especially the smaller ones more open to new artists. And those that are still open don't seem too excited about taking a risk on an unknown."

Formerly the life bread of the artist, brick-and-mortar galleries were dramatically affected by the downturn, and many of those that survived dispensed with frills, including promotional services for the artists they represented. The Great Recession offered no safety net, no equivalent to the 1930's Depression-era Works Process Administration (WPA) arts program to mitigate the blow to artists through the down years. This lack of security made us both feel the good fortune of Lise's acceptance even more. It made us hope.

The faster response time to gallery applications did nothing to lift the bewildering gallery mystique. Peter researched for hours on end and took great care to apply to those galleries where he perceived his work to fit. At least 85% did not respond to his inquiries at all. Another 10% replied with a "Great work but no thanks", which left the artist scratching his head about the *why* of it. There was occasionally an explanation like "We're not taking new artists" or "We have no room" or "You have no connection to the region", but responses of any kind were rare.

"You know, in your desperation to make sense of all this, you're losing studio time and you're going to drive yourself crazy," I said, looking over his shoulder at his latest research. "You might want to take this in small doses and just go paint. That way, when you do get a favorable response, you'll have work ready."

Difficult as it was to pull away, he did just that.

We flew out to New Jersey together to meet Lise in person. She was gracious, smart and tasteful, all of which were reflected in her elegant gallery display.

"Please frame everything in gold," she requested. "With uniform frames on the walls, buyers can focus on the art itself."

Looking at the gallery walls, the point was difficult to argue. Peter and I threw each other a sideways glance, then quickly looked down at our shoes. We'd already been through the school of hard knocks with framing. Peter's responsiveness to the preference of each Midwest gallery had left us with a mixed collection of expensive frames now collecting dust in the studio. None of this stock met Lise's criteria. The cost of the new frames along with that of the canvases, shipping, insurance and commission, left little to feed the painter.

Lise astutely intuited our strain and turned to Peter.

"Your prices are too low. Let's get them up where they belong," she said.

His eyes widened. Even at his lowest prices, he'd been told repeatedly in the Midwest market that he charged too much. Here was proof that he had finally landed in the right place.

As an afterthought, Lise added understandingly, with a smile at me, "You know, many artists I represent have a second job or a supporting partner, at least for a while."

Peter and I turned to each other in surprise. Until that moment, we'd thought our arrangement was rather unusual. The knowledge that other artists, too, didn't make all of their living from their art, at least at first, was at the same time a comfort and a hard truth.

When we left the gallery, Peter found a quiet moment to hug me with his thanks.

"Without you, none of this would be possible," he told me.

I drank it up.

In art, there is a "rule of thirds" theory that suggests the human eye naturally gravitates to measurable points, called "sweet spots", on a canvas. Lise's representation turned our eyes eastward again to the market sweet spot, in our estimation, for Peter's work. He still persisted in Midwestern venues and national art organizations and shows. He taught classes at Omaha's world class Joslyn Art Museum, contributed work to hospital fund raisers and even memorialized in paint the soon-to-be-demolished Rosenblatt Baseball Stadium that had hosted the College World Series for ages. Still, the undeniable reality was that Lise sold five paintings in six months. The sweet spot quickly became a focal point.

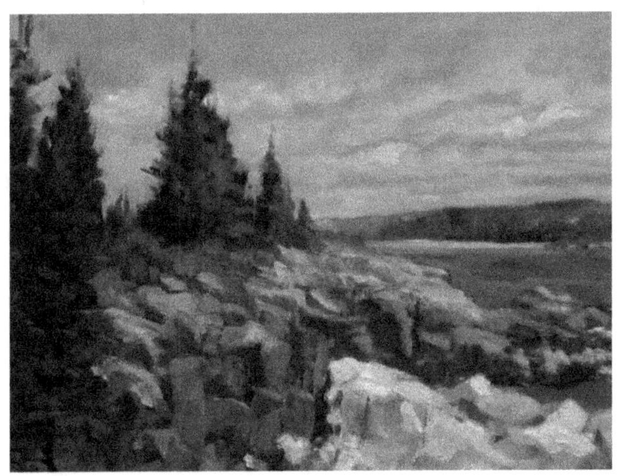

20

Lights and Shadows

*"It is a mistake to look too far ahead.
Only one link of the chain of destiny can be handled at a time."*
—Winston Churchill

Lise's gallery quickly became the highlight of Peter's budding career, and her sales were a boon. Like galleries of old, she advertised his work and arranged for private viewings by incognito collectors, one of whom purchased *Carafe Sur Rouge,* the painting that had merited exhibition at the International Guild of Realism show in Naples. We made several more trips to New Jersey to see Peter's work on display and to paint New Jersey scenes en plein air. As a consequence, his attraction to the East Coast, the "sweet spot", intensified, morphing from piqued interest to absolute absorption.

For the first time in our marriage, our respective views of the future diverged.

"All we have right now is one great gallery and a thumbnail sketch of a life somewhere along a 2000 mile stretch of coast. And we have obligations here," I reminded him. "At work and at home."

I was overseeing a huge renovation project at work. We had a parent in our care. We provided weekend lodging for our son and his wife while he was on Air Force Reserves duty as well as regular child care for our new grandson.

"Until we can see our way clear of all of this," I argued, "I can't imagine a life somewhere else."

Undeterred by my arguments, Peter pressed on, talking less in practical realities than in impassioned vagaries. He clearly had already framed out a new life of art-on-the-coast in his head, if only his partner could see it.

"Well," I declared, unmoved, "you're just going to have to dream for both of us."

My hesitation had to do with more than just responsibilities. At a time when many were still reeling from the economic downturn, we lived in a home that was almost paid for. I had a good job, and we'd made it through the Great Recession so far with relative ease. Our children lived nearby. We had made friends in the region. In short, we lived a life of abundance, and I filled with guilt whenever we talked about walking away from it all, particularly in this climate of uncertainty and loss.

"You could continue to build your career from here," I tested Peter's resolve. "We love this house, and we've put so much into it. Look at our garden! We could still be perfectly happy right here and travel for your landscape painting."

"Yes, we could," he concurred with underwhelming conviction.

My arguments were ineffectual. This was a full-blown, Peter-style launch. He could not suppress a heart and mind that were already out east, although he couldn't begin to articulate how or when the rest of him was going to get there. This visionary gap between us cast shadows over our partnership, our marriage and our direction. Conversations stopped short. Laughter was subdued. And I developed an edginess that made me jumpy and humorless. Peter became so immersed in destination research that I found it hard to remember the point of all this was to get closer to his art market. We simply weren't getting beyond the underpainting.

The East Coast is a pretty big expanse, and although we'd been lightly entertaining a return there for years, we'd never fixed a destination point. The only detail that never wavered was our desire to be near salt water.

"Not Jersey," I said firmly, when Peter pressed me on the topic. "We'd never be able to afford a place near enough to the water there. Plus, it's so crowded."

He began looking up and down the coast, quickly dismissing states with long, humid summers and populous beach areas. The elimination process still left a swath of varied coastline to explore, so it was not surprising that he zeroed in on what we knew.

"Nova Scotia would be perfect. We loved it there," he recalled, pulling up our old vacation photos.

I left him to his own devices.

On one narrow aspect of our future Peter and I could agree. Whether we stayed in Omaha or moved east, we wanted to live more simply. Our Cape Cod, having served as a nest for so many, was packed with accumulated belongings on all three floors.

"We could start downsizing right now," Peter suggested, grasping for something tangible—anything—that would get us working in the same direction again.

I dumbly nodded my consent, and we began to cast off possessions as if the answers to life could be found at the back of the attic, affording at least the illusion of forward motion. In the meantime, Peter painted industriously, and it did not escape me that, as we pared down household possessions, they were simply being supplanted by his burgeoning art work. In my mental estimation, it would be about an even swap at the end of the day.

As Peter and I danced out of step with one another through the ensuing months, other changes were brewing. After over a decade in our care, his mother decided to move east to be nearer the rest of the family. We were still processing her departure when our son's Reserve duty, and hence his regular monthly visits, abruptly ended, and he and his wife moved farther away. The last stroke came when our daughter quit her office job, and Peter reluctantly handed our grandson back to his mother, downgrading from regular daycare to occasional babysitter. Our full house had become an indistinct memory, as if layers of paint had been scraped away leaving only the ghost of past activity. The rhythm of our home recalibrated, and the house began to feel absurdly large and eerily empty.

"I keep looking over my shoulder as if I'm missing something," I told Peter.

"Well, you are," he answered simply.

Peter's enthusiasm for the coast intensified even more, if that was possible, in the months following the rapid contraction of our household. He pulled every able warm body into the search process. Heaving a bracing breath, I plunged into the family room where our son and daughter-in-law, visiting after a long hiatus, sat cross-legged on the floor amidst tea cups, open maps, and Nova Scotia real estate listings. Google Earth was up on the computer screen. The conversation was animated. Discoveries were being called out, and highlighted ads passed around the room. By this time, I'd taken to spectating quietly from the sidelines. It took far less energy than maintaining resistance.

Left to my own reflections, an unexpected idea flitted faintly across my mind. *Maine.* Sitting up straight, I offered it loudly to the room. "How about Maine?" Peter's head came up, and his eyes flashed. "Maine," I repeated with emphasis, looking straight at him. "It just popped into my head. We love Maine."

The idea felt so natural, I couldn't understand how we had skipped over this very desirable stretch of eastern coastline. Suddenly, I was the one expanding on the idea and getting into the spirit of the thing.

"Maine has a huge art community and a great variety of terrain for plein air landscapes. New England is full of realists. And being on this side of the border would make it easier to see the kids," I went on and on.

It was the first time I'd truly joined the process, and I just leapt into the thick of it. Everyone else froze in a momentary silence as they listened to my monologue, then excitedly kicked into a new gear. Before I knew it, I was crammed in front of the computer screen with the others clicking madly on possibilities. It had been a light bulb moment, and the idea felt more obvious the more we explored it.

From this strangely born suggestion, Peter began to cobble together an existence for us that contemplated every possible means of providing for ourselves. It was so nice to have him back on the planet and to be at ease again.

"What is this?" I asked as he brought several platters to the dinner table one night.

"Hot dogs!" he answered excitedly. "I bought every kind they had so we can find the best ones. Do you know how much you can make running a hot dog stand in the season? I've researched the costs and income potential. I could run the stand part-time and paint the rest of the time." He lowered his voice and said in earnest explanation, "I'll do anything to get out there."

How I loved this man.

Giggling, I selected a few dogs for my plate and scooped a pile of sauerkraut to embellish the taste test. There were large and small dogs of pork, chicken and beef, some organic, vegan or kosher and others not so much. We ate, critiqued and laughed our way through this meal, but I could not miss the deeper meaning of the exercise. Peter wanted to move east for art. He wanted this move so badly, he was willing to become a hot dog vendor. His humility, determination and restored pragmatism swiftly evaporated any remaining fog between us and reset the five-year plan to a phase we dubbed, simply, *Maine*. It also reinvigorated Peter in the studio. We were finally painting our way out of the shadows.

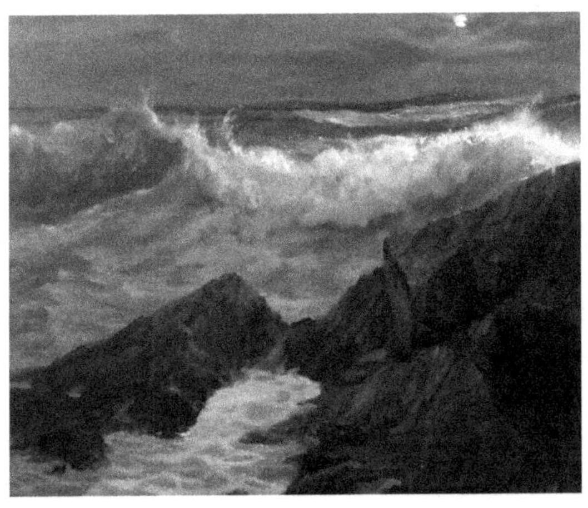

21

Art Opening

"Do not go where the path may lead;
go instead where there is no path and leave a trail."
—Ralph Waldo Emerson

"Look at this!"

Peter thrust a Craigslist ad in front of me as I walked in the door from work. *26 wooded acres in Downeast Maine* was circled several times with blue ink.

"Yes, but…"

"I've already talked to the owner," he rushed on before I found my voice. "I got a good feeling from her. We love the area. This property is within walking distance of the bay. Think about living near the bay! I think we should go look at it. Maybe this is the place!" His body was taut with energy as he walked about, gesturing and expounding on the possibilities. "It's in a kind of a micro-climate, a bit warmer planting zone. There's room for a huge garden and an orchard. We could build our own house there, a cabin in the woods. Oh, the painting possibilities will be endless! There's even room for the kids to build next door!" he concluded, as if this was the pièce de résistance.

He wasn't entirely off base.

As a general rule, I tried to make key decisions after careful research and a period of consideration, but Peter and I had a tacit agreement in our marriage to respect each other's intuition. We recognized, of course, that one person's intuitive flash is another person's moment of insanity, yet we'd followed each other's leadings in the past and never regretted it. Pragmatic as I was, unready as I was, I decided to trust Peter's brainwave about the property despite my own misgivings, just as he had embraced my insight about Maine. We spent the rest of the night on the internet and Google Earth studying the plot and environs and researching everything from employment to galleries.

In the course of a few days, we had tickets to Maine. In less than a week, we were traipsing across a breath-taking wooded property blanketed with snow with a wonderful stand of cedars, a large blueberry patch and a long slope warmed by the sun. A few hours later, I watched detachedly as my hand scratched out an earnest deposit check and extended it to the owner. I was so overcharged I was insensible.

"What did we just do?" I asked Peter, wringing my hands as the owner pulled away. "I don't think it falls in the prudent category."

"Maybe not," he replied, "but it felt like the right thing to do."

Did it? I did not share Peter's certainty. I had relied on his intuition, my own being entirely out of service. The only thing playing in my head was static.

"Anyway, land is a good investment," he reasoned belatedly. "If we don't get out here, we can sell it."

I looked at him blankly, awed at his self-possession after having committed a significant portion of our savings to this property.

"Our primary goal is your art success," I repeated mechanically, staring straight ahead.

The words sounded hollow, even to me. Caught up in Maine's beauty and this whirlwind decision, I wasn't sure I knew what the goal was any longer. And buying the place brought my deepest reservation to the surface: Would uprooting ourselves to live on the East Coast really make a substantive difference to Peter's art career? I honestly had no idea. What I did know was that, standing by the bay, I'd never felt more at home.

As surreal as the property purchase felt, once we touched ground in Omaha, it affected both of us like electric shock therapy. There was something incredibly mobilizing about that pile of rock and sticks in Maine we could now call our own. Our first action was to list our Cape Cod for sale. Apart from memories, what did we have to lose? As we watched the realtor walk to her car, we felt a little foolish having listed in the immediate wake of the Great Recession.

"It's better to err than to regret inaction," I asserted in our defense.

"And it only takes one buyer," we reminded one another philosophically as we accelerated our downsizing and began to knock off minor repairs.

In the evenings, we occasionally revisited the Downeast property on Google Earth, and I half-heartedly poked around for jobs in the area. At this point, every stroke was tentative, but at least some paint had hit the canvas.

The downside of the property purchase was a newfound dichotomy in our lives. Everything we did was now weighed and measured against its impact not only on today but also on a nebulous future seventeen hundred miles away. The present and future collided daily, complicating even the smallest decisions.

"How many art supplies should I stock?"

"What kind of car should we buy?"

"Do we really need a new freezer?"

Trekking a household across half the country demanded financial and logistical economies and lots of forethought. This straddling of two worlds was really taxing, and it took our combined efforts to maintain a proper balance.

Peter continued to paint still lifes but, with the prospect of an eastward move, the draw of landscapes—seascapes to be more precise—was irresistible. We made two more trips to Maine the next year, in spring to identify homebuilders and in the fall to focus on art itself, from which he built a collection of studies. Plein air painting, quite the rage by this time, was quickly becoming Peter's passion as well.

In Maine, the challenge wasn't to *find* material but to *choose* from among a myriad of gorgeous scenes in the short time our vacations allowed. He tirelessly hauled his gear from site to site while I trailed behind with a backpack of food, books and journals—OK, yes, and a little wine—and then plopped down contentedly behind the easel to watch his progress. As I followed his brush work by the bay at low tide, the final vestige of plaguing hesitation suddenly lifted from me. His obvious energy, the plentiful subject matter, his comfort with the landscape—all this came together, and it struck me clearly that his presence on the coast was, in fact, quite material to his painting. How could I ever have questioned this?

On our way back to the motel, Peter abruptly veered the rental car into a parking lot.

"We've passed this place enough times now. I want to stop in and check it out."

It was a combination interior design showcase and art gallery with a tasteful, upscale selection. Peter handed his card to the owner, a smart, personable woman with exquisite taste and great aspirations for her gallery.

"Peter! I know you! I know your work through a friend!" she exclaimed instantly.

Peter could not hide his surprise. We didn't know many people in Maine, but it turned out that a contractor we'd met had passed Peter's card along to her. After hearing about our land purchase and plans to build, she took on his representation.

"You just never know what forces are quietly at work in your life," I remarked dazedly as we climbed back into the car.

"No kidding," Peter answered as he sat staring at the steering wheel for a few moments in happy bewilderment.

There's a spark of excitement when you twist off the cap of a shiny new tube of paint. Infinite possibilities are hidden in that tube, and the first stream of fresh paint almost shouts its potential. The color looks almost alien, as if you're discovering it for the first time, and it releases a stimulating whiff of paint odor into your nostrils. Our land purchase was like this first squeeze of fresh paint, clean, bright and full of promise. The closest I can come to this analogy as a writer is the gentle crack and delicious smell of fresh paper as you break open a new journal.

We had zeroed in on a destination.

Peter had art representation in both Maine and New Jersey.

We had hope.

All that remained was practical means.

"This is the crux of the thing," I reminded Peter, "the way we'll finally know the move is the right thing to do. We need an indication on the ground that living in Maine is possible. The Omaha house has to sell, and then either a job for me or heightened success in art or both."

I looked over at him. In this moment, we felt close, so very close, to the coveted sweet spot.

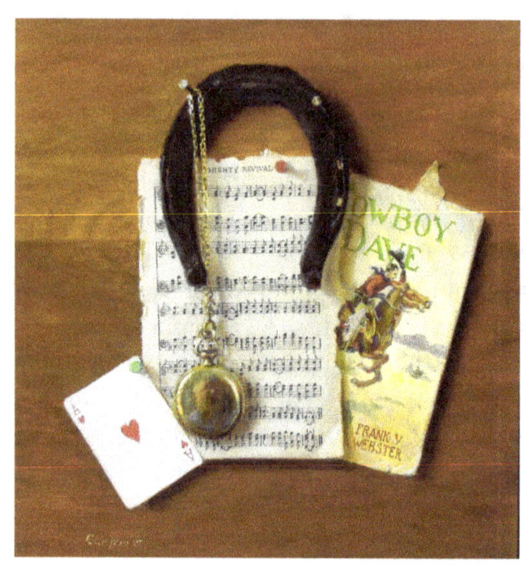

Cowboy Dave, oil, Peter Yesis

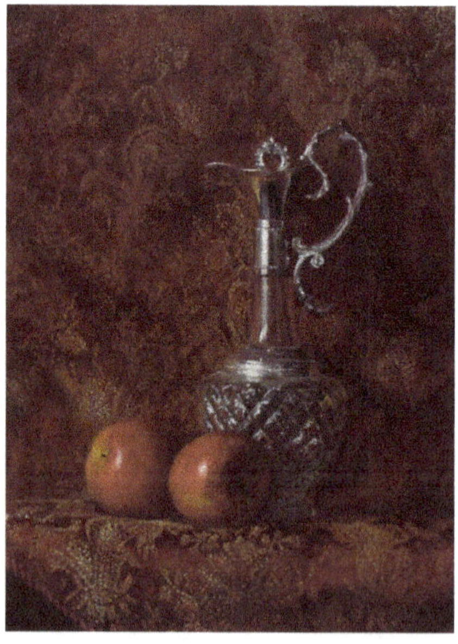

Carafe sur Rouge, oil, Peter Yesis

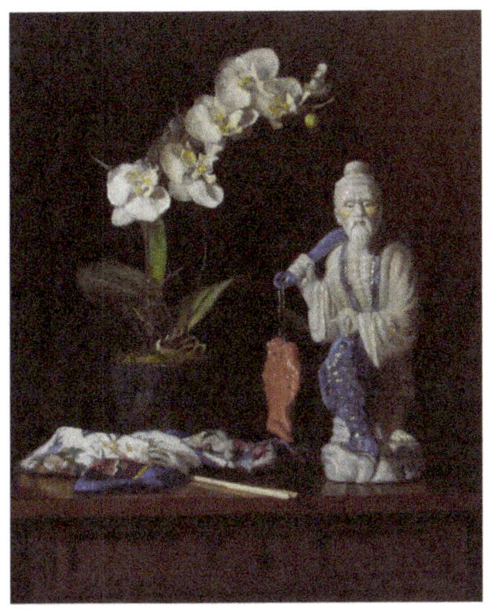

For Miyako, oil, Peter Yesis

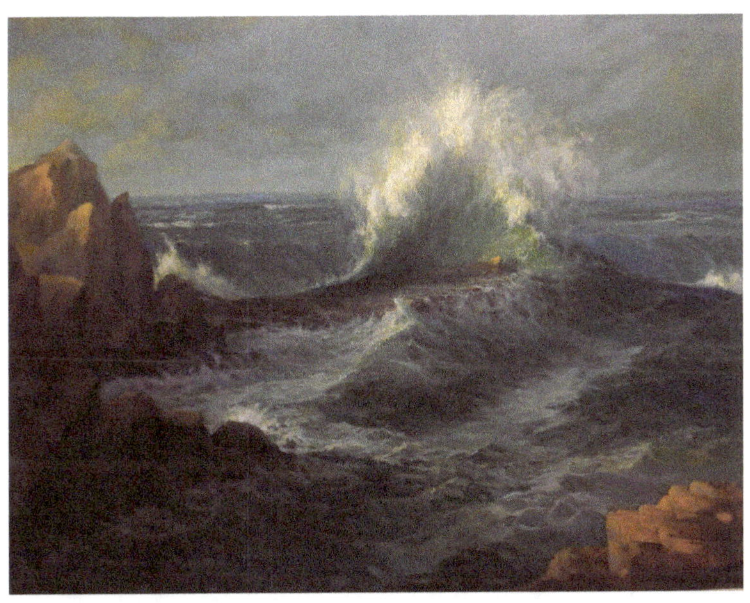

Crescendo, oil, Peter Yesis

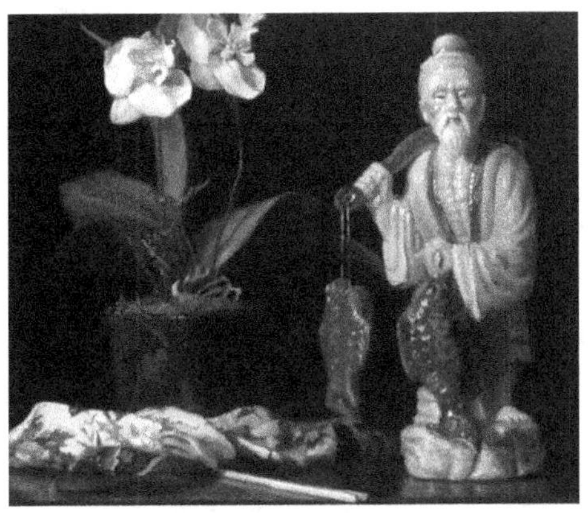

22

Artist's Block

"Grief is in two parts. The first is loss. The second is the remaking of life."
—Anne Roiphe

Happy as I was for Peter's art prospects, I had to admit that a part of me had begun to chafe inside. The idea of moving to an idyllic place like Maine with no change in my own day was unsettling. I wanted to be more involved in art and to have some creative space of my own. I wanted to write. Until we'd purchased the Downeast land, I'd really not differentiated the collective gnawing of these desires from the other stressors in our life. Now, as we inched closer to our goal, I realized that moving to Maine had become, for me, about more than Peter's art; it was about my hopes, too. Each time we visited our new place, bouncing playfully on the soft mosses, inhaling the smell of pines and saltwater, I felt my job aspirations downshift a notch. The more quickly we got to Maine, the sooner I could begin to forge a new path of my own.

Peter took my hand across the breakfast table and looked intently into my eyes, reading me, as he always did, like a book.

"Once we get settled, it'll be your turn. We've been planning only for my art, but this move has to be about both of us."

I stared at him. At times like this, our relationship bordered on telepathy. He gestured to the open journal on the table.

"I'm so glad you've found writing," he said encouragingly.

"It isn't much," I answered candidly, not the least bit impressed with what I'd put down on paper.

"What's important now is that you build the muscle," he reminded me, "and record your creative ideas."

I leaned back against the chair, soaking up his life-breathing words. It was Peter's turn to coach.

"You should get as much from this move as I do," he added firmly.

My eyes began to fill with tears at the prospect. I quickly suppressed them. I couldn't let myself go down that path, not yet. I'd never be able to handle the hard road ahead if I was already curling my toes in the sand. I'd rejected the hot dog stand and Peter's other ideas for his employment, so I would remain the primary breadwinner for the foreseeable future. It was only fair. I'd had a ten-year sabbatical to do what I loved. His had been cut short, dashed by the economic crisis, and he needed time to start over. My dream would remain on the back burner for now. It was reassuring to know it was ready to fire up when the time was right.

"You painted in your off hours while still working in engineering," I reminded Peter. "I'll just keep writing whenever I can, and someday…" I let the thought dangle in the air.

"Yes, but someday *soon*," he emphasized.

Not a week after we landed back in Omaha, lungs full of sea air, we sat breathless on the living room couch. From the looks of our daughter's expectant belly, our first granddaughter would not be long coming into the world and would then be instantly whisked from our lives. Our daughter sat in the rocker, cheeks a rosy pink, with our toddler grandson playing at her side as she relayed the news. Our son-in-law had been offered a job, a promotion, out east. It was too good to pass up. The family would relocate shortly after the baby's birth.

My eyes ran over our carefully child-proofed living room, the strewn books and toys, the blankets and pillows and even the little hand smudges on the large picture window. Peter and I had been integral to the life of this growing family and we had literally rearranged our lives for them. There was no denying the news was a blow. In stoic parent style, we offered congratulations and talked excitedly with our daughter about her hopes and plans. As she pulled away, we waved good-bye in heartbreak.

"I had no idea how much their proximity really meant until she told us," I admitted to Peter tearfully.

He just shook his head.

Anyone more clear-headed than us, which was just about everyone, saw this new development quite differently.

"You would have left them anyway when you moved to Maine. Don't you see that this means you have one less tie to Omaha?" our son and daughter-in-law argued artfully over Skype. "You should go to Maine."

"We haven't sold the house yet," I countered. "And I'll need a job out there. We can't just pick up and go."

Two months later, we walked our daughter and grandchildren to the airport gate, putting on our best you-are-free-to-choose-your-own-life faces until we waved them out of sight.

"My hands still smell like baby lotion," I choked to Peter as we walked slowly back to the car.

"Please don't tell me you'll never wash them again."

He glanced over at me grinning. Behind the levity was a pair of sad eyes.

"This separation is bad enough," I complained on the way home, "but you have to admit the final rub is that it is *our* dream to move east, and just about everybody is moving there except us. First your mother. Now the kids."

I did wash my hands, though I made Peter leave our grandson's handprints on the picture window for weeks. Grief took a temporary toll on both of us. I cried off and on and spilled my tears into my journal. Peter fared worse. Gout flared up in his foot, and he had to sit awkwardly at the easel with one leg elevated.

"Maybe you need a week of naps and Cheerios," I attempted

a joke as I adjusted his foot pillow.

He sat up sharply and winced in pain, but even pain could not resurrect his concentration, and he remained adrift for weeks. I watched him become caught up in beginning new pieces and overpainting others so that very few finished works were emerging during this downtime, with the singular exception of a still life entitled *Top Shelf*, which was juried into the Salon International show.

Normally, Peter would have taken on another challenge to pull himself together, but before he could do so, he was jolted into action by the terrible tsunami that hit Miyako City, Japan. The shockwave of this news ran through his frame and instantly restored his perspective. His lethargy was replaced by horror at the tremendous loss, which he channeled into the stunning still life *For Miyako*, a memorial to the victims and a tribute to the survivors.

Clarity restored and gout fading, the re-energized artist jumped into seascapes, boats and rocky coasts, leaning particularly on Homer for inspiration.

"Do I smell blueberries?" I sniffed as I dropped into the basement for a studio visit.

"Blueberry tea," he answered, grinning. "I'm painting Maine, so I thought it was fitting."

He bent over a large box with a box cutter.

"What's in there?" I asked.

He shrugged at me sheepishly.

"A new plein air box with a tripod. I thought it was time to replace the old duct-taped version, you know, to celebrate our new property. It's part of the Maine plan. I'll be doing more plein air painting out there."

I did a mental count. One artist. Four easels and counting with this new purchase. We were downsizing everywhere but in the studio.

"You can drink all the blueberry tea you want," I said irritably one afternoon, "but that'll be as close to Maine as we get unless this house sells. I know the market is slow, but to have no lookers at all?"

We'd bought the Downeast property in the fall and listed immediately. It was now early spring.

Peter called the realtor.

"The economy is still bad," she explained. "Omaha didn't have a housing bubble, but we're feeling the pressure. Buyers can't get loans."

In fact, the downturn was still midstream, and the harsh reality was that the country was headed for a bank bailout, not a homeowner bailout. Not only were houses not selling; foreclosure signs were popping up around the neighborhood.

"At least we didn't have to face that nightmare," I spoke my relief aloud.

As if synchronized with the housing market, Peter's art sales hit an all-time low.

"Without the New Jersey and Maine galleries, last year would have been a complete bust. This year looks no better," he reflected dispiritedly. "Maybe it's a sign."

"It's a sign that times are hard right now," I answered. "It's harder to make a living of any kind. Let's just stay focused. It'll pick up."

I didn't dare suggest a time for this uptick when even the best economists had no idea. Summer and then fall came and went with no material upswing in art sales, nor any change in house activity.

"A whole year has gone by," Peter lamented. "Housing prices have dropped. Buyers are scarce. We have to try a new tack."

We canceled the realty contract, and Peter pounded a FOR SALE BY OWNER sign on the lawn while I listed on a for-sale-by-owner web site.

"At least this way we're not entirely shutting the door," Peter contended, "and, if it sells, we won't have to pay a commission."

One evening that winter, Peter's phone rang.

"It's Lise," he mouthed to me, and turned to take the call.

Maybe she's sold another one, I thought hopefully, watching for Peter's reaction. After an unusually lengthy and sober conversation, I began to fear she was discontinuing his representation, although I could not understand why. Peter's work was moving in her gallery. He hung up the phone frowning. Matters were far worse.

"Lise is closing the gallery," he announced sadly. "She's really sick. Cancer. It doesn't sound good."

We both stood for a while in stunned silence looking at the

disconnected phone as if it would somehow ring again with different news. Lise had become a pillar, a confidante, an advisor. We could not imagine the art world or ours without her. The following June, she died a premature death, leaving friends, family and art associates saddened and bereft of her grace, her class and her passion for art. In death as in life, Lise's influence would be deeply felt.

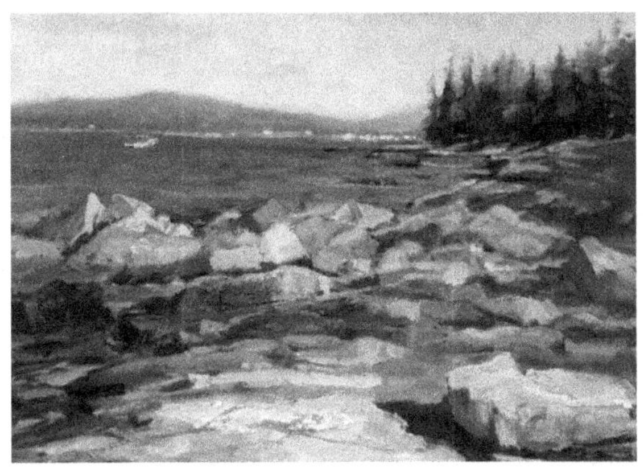

23

Toning It Down

"What day is it?"
"It's today," squeaked Piglet.
"My favorite day," said Pooh.
— A.A. Milne

If ever I'd wondered how Lise's death would affect Peter, I would not have to wait long to find out. I came home from work to find him trying on his old work boots, the same worn out, old leather ones he'd retired and memorialized in his daily painting six years ago. I looked my question at him.

"I've taken a job as a landscaping foreman," he said simply.

"*What?* When? Why? What about your art?"

I objected in as many ways as I could in a single breath, choking on the lump forming in my throat. I had made just as much investment in his art as Peter. I wasn't willing to throw in the towel without a fight.

"I can't just sit around painting if I have only one place to show the work and hardly a name for myself," he told me flatly. "It's irresponsible. I'll keep painting on the side to feed the Maine gallery

111

while I earn money for the new house. In the meantime, I'll keep looking for more galleries and getting my name out there however I can while we wait for the market to turn around."

He spun his decision sanguinely. I studied him carefully. What a relief to hear that, despite all the disappointments and his profound sadness of late, Peter was not quitting. In the last year or so, he'd been turned around like a kid in a game of pin-the-tail-on-the-donkey and now had simply started moving in the first direction his boots would take him. I decided I admired his pluck and gave him his head. Anyway, sometimes the way through is to go around.

The landscaping job went fine for the first week, aside from some very sore muscles. By the second week, Omaha was experiencing sweltering temperatures in excess of 100 degrees. Peter left one morning and returned home later visibly thinner, his skin hanging from his face. My heart jumped in panic at the sight of him. I shoved glass after glass of water at him, then forced him to eat a high-calorie supper, all the while hiding my fears behind admonishments.

"You have to increase your water and calorie intake if you're going to work like a crazy teenager in this heat!"

We reworked his diet to fit his new needs, but I didn't think the prognosis was good for the long haul.

"Why don't you look for something in engineering?" I urged. "You can make two to three times this hourly rate doing engineering, and then you could work part-time for the same amount of income and paint more."

"I've left engineering. I don't want to go back," he said in a pleading voice.

How well I understood. In the end, it wasn't my prodding that decided him. Despite the new regime, he began coming home so physically depleted, evening painting was entirely out of the question. The final blow was a severe skin reaction to the landscaping chemicals.

By August, Peter was back in engineering with a schedule that got him home early enough to paint.

"I know this isn't the way you wanted it to go," I said comfortingly, "but, at least this way, if our opportunity ever comes, I know I won't be going to Maine with a sick partner."

Once again, I found myself working alongside an artist

masquerading as an engineer. I freely admit that I didn't mind the financial help Peter's income gave us. He fiddled with a computer design of our Maine house all the while he socked money away to pay for it. Still, I was saddened to see art take a back seat and said so.

"I'm painting almost as much as I was before I took this job," he reassured me. "When we're not terribly busy at work," he looked at me slyly, pulling a mysterious wad of paper scraps from his pants pocket, "I use this." It was a little homemade sketch book. "I made it from office scrap and keep it with me all the time. It's small, so it's discreet. If they don't have work for me, I pull out my book and start sketching."

I had to turn my face away. Peter had gone from painting openly to his heart's content to stealing sketches at the office in between assignments. When I turned back to him, I was surprised to see he was smiling widely.

"Look," he invited.

The first few pages were sketches of his co-workers and areas around the office, but the following pages were full of seascapes.

"They're all in my brain," he said proudly. "I remember scenes of Maine I loved and scratch out thumbnails for future paintings. It's like a diary so I have a head start on composition when I get back in the studio. And I paint every day when I come home while you're still at work. I'm even playing with water colors in addition to oils just to shake things up and keep them interesting."

My jaw opened, then snapped shut again. I could look at Peter as an artist reduced to scribbling on paper scraps or an artist determined to produce regardless of circumstances. I chose the latter, glad that once outed, there was no putting the artist back in the paint box.

With no other choice, we hunkered down in our comfortable Cape Cod to wait out another Nebraska winter and the languishing economy, though with a new philosophy: live in the now. The concept of mindfulness, of living well in the moment, was not so mainstream back then, but we figured it was the only way to remain sane. Looking too far ahead was just not fruitful and it drained us. We both kept our mindful heads down all winter, working, saving, downsizing and seizing the day.

Another spring arrived with not one call of interest about the house since Peter had pounded the for-sale sign into the ground the prior fall. As soon as the ground thawed, he yanked the sign from the lawn, muttering, "It's too depressing to keep looking at it."

It had been two and half years since we'd purchased the Downeast Maine property and initially listed the Cape Cod. Yet, here we were in the Midwest with no end in sight. We weren't defeated but we were definitely ready to put the whole Maine plan in mothballs.

"Maybe we should just let the whole thing go right now," I threw at Peter almost breathlessly. "Stop longing for a future that isn't materializing. If circumstances ever change, we'll spring into action then."

I watched him as he sat in silent reflection for a few moments, then lifted his face to me.

"Good idea," was all he said.

Whatever it meant to Peter's art career, whatever it meant to my hopes, Maine was relegated to the back room like an unfinished painting that would be reprised the moment we knew what to do with it. That night, we slept the most peaceful sleep we'd slept in a long time.

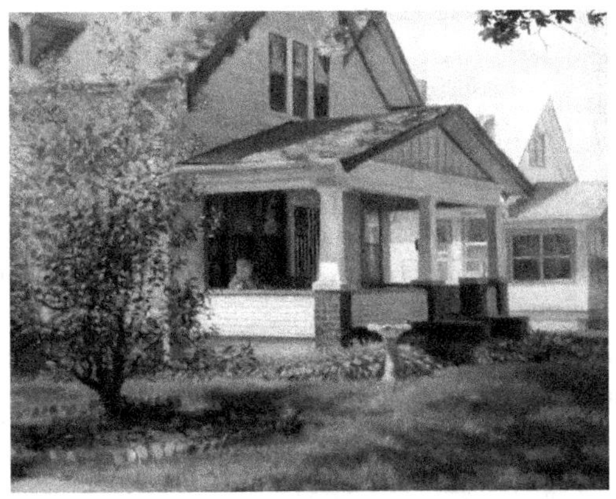

24

Creative Release

"All the art of living lies in a fine mingling of letting go and holding on."
—Havelock Ellis

What did we feel the morning after we let go of our dream? *Complete release.*

No more juggling two worlds. No more pressure to complete house repairs or a new house design. No more fretting that the house hadn't sold. Adios to job hunting. We would simply live well where we were planted for the foreseeable future and got right to it, spending the weekend in relaxing pursuits. By Sunday afternoon, the house was strewn with the residues of our creative rush: fresh painting attempts, full journal pages and a major bread-baking bonanza. The only serious work to be done was washing dishes and folding laundry.

"We should probably get this place at least reasonably cleaned up," I said finally, nodding my head in the direction of the dishes and glancing at the clock. "Work tomorrow."

"Yeah," Peter agreed, turning on the hot water to wash the dishes and bakeware.

Around three o'clock in the afternoon, Peter's phone rang. He answered and listened for a few minutes. A shadow of confusion passed over his face. I frowned in concern. This didn't look good, and we'd had enough bad news lately.

"Hold on, will you, please?" he asked the caller ever so politely.

By his tone, it was obvious this wasn't someone we knew. What stranger would be calling on a late Sunday afternoon? If it had been a marketing call, he'd have hung up already.

After muting the phone, he whispered as if the caller could still hear, "Is our house still for sale?"

"What?"

"Is our house still for sale?" he repeated the words in slow, emphatic succession. "There's somebody who wants to look at it."

"We took the For Sale sign down." I stated the obvious, glancing through the window to the lawn.

"We didn't take the web posting down, though," he continued. "She found us online. She says she went to Zillow and clicked on our house by mistake, then decided she'd like to see it."

There was a long silence as Peter and I inwardly processed this unexpected development and debated the caller's question against our very fresh decision to let go.

"What could it hurt?" I concluded noncommittally. "We haven't had a single looker, so I can't see how we can decline the one and only person who's ever shown interest. Anyway, her feedback might be useful someday."

"That's what I'm thinking, too. We don't have to agree to anything."

I paused.

"Is this a test of our resolve or of our openness to being wrong?" I threw at Peter, running my hand through my hair.

"I guess we'll find out." He relayed the answer to the caller, hung up the phone, turned to me and said, "They're on their way over."

"Now?"

"Yes, now." He added, "Of course, they may not even show up."

"No, they may not," I agreed, thinking this was the more likely scenario.

We walked together from room to room assessing the fallout from our devil-may-care weekend of liberation. The place was pretty messy, at least by our standards. At any other time, one of us would have grabbed the vacuum while the other frantically tried to restore order. Not this time. If this was the buyer for us, she would see through the chaos. If not, so be it. Letting the whole thing go again in my mind was so very uplifting. I was too tired from the waiting, the preparing, the hoping. Let the universe handle it. Anyway, the more probable outcome was that the caller would just not show. Peter leisurely turned the music volume up and stuck his hands back in the dish water while I quietly resumed folding laundry.

The ring of the doorbell twenty minutes later startled both of us out of our silent musings.

"My God, she's actually here," I marveled in astonishment.

We opened the brick-red front door to a young twenty-something with a face full of piercings and traces of blue coloring in her hair, her father and a realtor-friend. The clean freak in me couldn't help but offer an apology for the clutter, however feeble and insincere. They indifferently shrugged it off and proceeded to go over the entire house and grounds quite thoroughly, asking dozens of questions. Peter ran to retrieve from the recesses of the closet the information binder we'd prepared about the house when we'd first listed it for sale by owner. He wiped the dust off with his sleeve and brought it out to the visitors, who flipped through it with avid curiosity. We saw them out, shrugged at one another and returned to our business. We'd been waiting too long for a buyer to get excited about the first and only one in the door. And the one-eighty we'd taken on Friday was working out quite nicely, thank you very much.

We'd left everything to the universe, and the universe appeared at our door on Tuesday morning in the form of the realtor-friend bearing a signed offer. After almost three years without even a single call of interest, the only potential buyer to see it had extended an offer on the Cape Cod. Where was Guinness?

"We said it would only take one," Peter laughed incredulously, handing the contract to me as I walked in the door, having left work early when I got the news.

In our hands was a chance to take a material step toward the dream we had so unceremoniously closeted. I flipped the pages over as if questioning the contract's authenticity.

"I guess sometimes you just have to get out of your own way," I offered philosophically. If we accepted this deal, we would have sixty days to make some repairs and vacate. "If we take it, we're either hypocrites or nuts," I owned, then hesitated. "The thing is, though, we'd be free…free to look ahead." I was overwhelmed with emotion at the thought of it. Peter bear-hugged me in response. "Best to keep this to ourselves," I cautioned.

"Yeah. No one would believe it anyway," he answered.

We accepted the offer.

Sixty days did not leave time to examine our own sanity or even to wait until our heads stopped spinning. We made a plan of action to get everything ready for closing, pack our stuff and find a rental pronto. "This is really happening," I said aloud again and again more to myself than to Peter. He stuck his head out of the attic door, perspiration running down his face, and grinned broadly.

Our packing frenzy was punctuated by a minor art crisis. Some months ago, I had convinced Peter to pull his old work from the walls of his studio and set it aside. He'd progressed so rapidly even in the last three years since we'd bought the Maine property that his older paintings, although not very old, were clearly the work of days gone by.

"All around you is your past," I'd reasoned with him. "If you want your work to get stronger, you have to surround yourself with things that make you reach."

He'd bought the argument and cleared the studio walls. He now sat frozen in contemplation next to that very pile of old paintings and an open moving box.

I stepped over and said, "You can't rescue every painting attempt or you'll lose track of where you really want to go. Look at Monet. He discarded piles of unworthy paintings. Be selective."

He bravely took on the challenge.

"All this packing is fine," I fretted nervously, as I rolled up another glass in newspaper, "but what are we going to do if we don't find a place to live?"

Our plan was to take a rental in Omaha until we had a house and means in Maine. We searched continuously online and took every opportunity to drive up and down the streets looking for a rental sign. Rentals appeared and disappeared overnight, so you had to be quick.

Just a few weeks before closing, our nerves were beginning to fray, and we turned again to the few unappealing, undersized apartments we'd found in other areas of the city.

"I'd have loved to stay in the same neighborhood if we could have," I sighed disappointedly. "All the kids play outside here, like we did when we were kids. You don't see much of that anymore."

Just as we'd begun to resign ourselves to life in a box, Peter found, just two blocks from our Cape Cod, a tiny, 1940-something two-bedroom that had just been vacated. The property manager was pounding the For Rent sign into the lawn when Peter drove by. He stopped, took a cursory tour and ran home with the paperwork. The place was exactly what we needed. In rapid succession, we signed the lease, jammed our stuff into the little rental house and gave a final farewell to the Cape Cod.

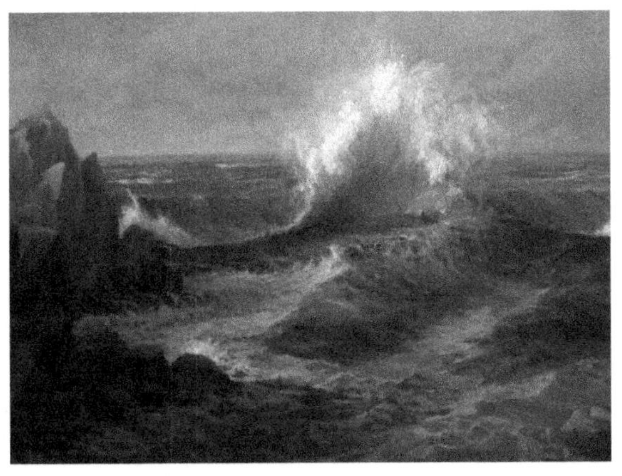

25

Sizing

"I dream my painting and then I paint my dream."
—Vincent van Gogh

We forcibly crammed the last moving box into the tiny basement of the rental house, now filled floor to ceiling except for a narrow passageway leading to the washer and dryer. Peter had to push a few things back tightly so we could fully open and close the basement door. It was like trying to shut an overflowing suitcase by sitting on the lid. We'd gone from 2400 square feet with ample storage to 900 square feet and almost none. The bulk of our belongings would remain packed in the basement. There was no other way we could fit in the tiny living area upstairs.

The upper rooms were bursting with furniture and the minimal household goods necessary to live, eat, sleep and paint. Each time Peter and I attempted to pass each other in a tight spot, we did a sort of turn to get by, giggling like a couple of kids on the dance floor.

"Look at the bright side," he said sensibly as he dramatically released me from a ballroom spin. "No matter how small our new house in Maine is, it'll feel like a palace after this."

The second bedroom of the rental doubled as Peter's studio. It was barely large enough to hold the trundle bed and dresser, but Peter somehow managed to squeeze in his easel, chair, palette table and supplies in such a way that he could work happily for hours at a time. He now invariably carried a tiny notebook he could pocket and take anywhere. In such a tiny place, it was fitting, I thought, that Peter continued his space-saving thumbnail sketches, even as we traveled again to the great Wisconsin North Woods.

He began to sketch out on canvas more Northwoods landscapes and also a few seascapes he'd held in reserve while we had been concentrating on the house sale and move. In the evenings, he watched video after video of breaking waves on the internet to make sure his water representations would be accurate. I swore I could smell saltwater from the couch, and the scent of his blueberry tea wafted from the studio doorway through the little house.

One evening, I came home to find a completed eighteen-by-twenty-four study of a huge ocean wave on the easel.

"Wow. When did you finish that?"

"I had most of it done before we moved. It's only a study," he answered. "Like it? It's from one of the sketches I drew at work in my little scrapbook."

You could have knocked me over with a feather. I couldn't believe he'd accomplished such a work in the midst of all the chaos and from a tiny image in his scrapbook, no less.

"I'm going to need help with a title, though."

Ah. Normal was finally re-emerging from all the upheaval, and She-Who-Must-Not-Be-Named had not lost her Chief of Titling job in the transition.

We continued with our jobs and our plans and headed into yet another Nebraska winter in a house so small we could carry on a conversation with each other from any other room. There was a real upside to the undersized rental. With one bath, a tiny kitchen, no garden and most of our possessions packed away, there was far less to maintain and nothing for us, as tenants, to repair. For the first time in memory, Peter and I had the precious commodity of time, and we used it wisely. Peter painted industriously. I had the luxury to write for hours and began transferring some of my material to the computer.

By this time, I had filled over a dozen journals, without counting notebooks about art marketing, and had developed three distinct storylines that I hoped to develop, plus a smattering of other ideas.

"Ready to hear some more?" I invited Peter as I stretched out on the couch, a convenient six feet from the studio door, while he painted.

He turned down the music and listened as I read excerpts aloud, noting his suggestions. Where this was all going to go, I had no idea, but I was thoroughly enjoying the ride.

By now, I could envision living in Maine so well that I was already picking out colors for our new, though not yet fully designed, place. And, in our good fortune between the Cape Cod sale and Peter's engineering job, that new place would almost be paid for. Peter tinkered off and on with the house design between office and studio work, idle pencil tucked behind his ear in old-fashioned engineering style as he worked the mouse.

"I can't figure out where to put the piano."

He leaned back, put his hands behind his head and furrowed his brow. I felt a stab in my heart. We'd bought a beautiful console piano when our kids were still toddlers, and it had taken years to pay off. I'd played it actively in the early years and had even taken advanced lessons but had let my skills go over the last decade. My playing days were over, plain and simple, yet I'd not yet been able to let the beloved instrument go. We'd paid extra to haul it to our little rental house where it now sat, neglected and collecting dust, on one end of the sun porch.

"We'll have to sell it," I told Peter heavily.

He twisted around toward me.

"Really? Are you sure? I know we can find space for it."

He turned determinedly back to the screen.

"It makes no sense to keep it if it is never played," came my practical response. "Even the kids aren't around to play it anymore. After the holidays, I'll post it on Craigslist," I committed firmly. There was a reflective pause. "Letting that piano go is key to our future," I asserted, ignoring my own pun. "Nothing will happen until it's sold."

I came home one evening to find a forty-by-sixty-inch canvas leaning half in and half out of the doorway to the tiny bedroom studio, a dramatic change from thumbnails and small studies.

"Do you have to get this expansive in this little house?" I asked. "Seriously?"

I peered around the canvas from the hallway, seeing no way to add my own presence to the already tightly packed room.

"Look at the scene," Peter countered, pointing to his smaller ocean wave study. "It's big in every sense of the word, so it needs a large canvas. It's the biggest canvas I've ever bought."

No kidding. I could no longer claim he was afraid of painting large after this. I took a careful look at the study. Peter was right. There was force and reach in that composition. I could feel my arms itching to make great swings in the air at the feeling of it, like an orchestra conductor. It needed room.

Maybe it was my subconscious piano angst bursting forth, maybe not, but I exclaimed, "*Crescendo*! Call it *Crescendo*!" And he did.

Living small doesn't mean you have to think small.

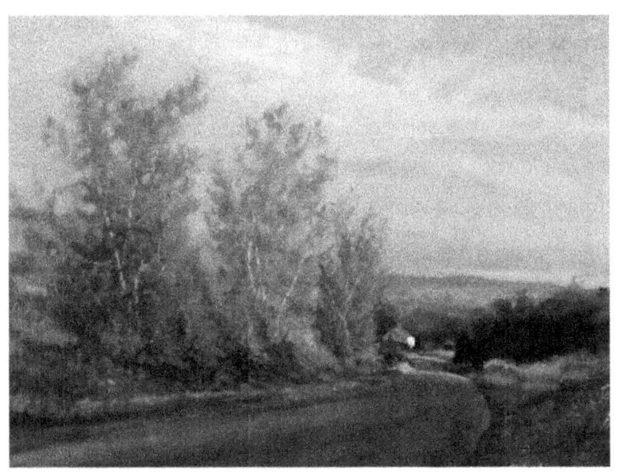

26

Art Essentials

*"To live as an artist requires hard work or
some extraordinary good fortune to come your way."*
—William Boyd

The piano sold in January to a family with a six-year-old whose face glowed with anticipation. The next day, I stood in the doorway absentmindedly holding a check in my hand as the instrument was loaded onto the truck. This sale wasn't about the money; it was about making room for something new. Any grief I felt was mollified by my anticipation of what would come in its wake.

"It's gone," I said wistfully to Peter as the truck rounded the corner, then added with interest, "but I wonder what's to come."

He did not laugh at my premonition. Instead, he stood with me in the empty space where the instrument had resided, wondering in tandem if, in the upcoming days, my piano prophesy would hold true.

By late winter, the magnificent *Crescendo* painting was finished, a huge leap forward for Peter in subject matter, skill and size. A southern Maine gallery invited Peter to show the piece at a July exhibit.

"What an honor," I said excitedly.

"Yeah, it really is," he agreed, then hesitated. "Now I have to figure out how to get this thing out there." This would be a shipping bill for the record books.

We had reached that frustrating mid-point like when you've excitedly blocked in a painting you anticipate will be fabulous but have to put your brushes down to wait for the first layer of paint to dry. The tension in the interval between the initial inspiration and the desire for the final product is tortuous. As if to add to it, my job entered a period of heavy demand. The budding writer in me screamed for attention, and it took an exercise of sheer will to suppress it during my long work days.

Peter picked up the job-hunting mantle and presented me with his findings every night when I got home.

"I really want you to be able to concentrate on art in Maine, but for myself, well…I'd really like something else or at least something…less," I repeated like a broken record, as if he couldn't already see this for himself. I enjoyed business and was challenged by it, but there can be too much of a good thing.

Not wanting to falsely raise my spirits, he also secretly began to look for small cottages in Maine.

"You can go there to rest," he later explained when I found him out, "while I work here until we find a better way."

"But I don't want to live apart from you," I protested, touched to the core.

"I don't want that either," he admitted, "but you obviously could use a rest."

One evening, Peter greeted me in the garage doorway as I pulled in. He reached into the car, grabbed my bags and headed for the door, urging me over his shoulder, "Hurry up. You won't believe what I found!"

Intrigued, I followed right on his heels. He hastily dumped my things on the couch and pulled me over to the computer.

"Tell me what's wrong with this place."

He pointed to a real estate listing of a ranch house surrounded by six acres of trees and sitting about 200 feet off a lakeside road. He stood next to me, palpably anxious for my reaction as I scrolled through the details and photos. The nine-year-old structure had a great room, two bedrooms, an alcove, two baths and radiant floor heat.

I turned to him.

"It's really close to the design you've been creating," I observed.

"That's what struck me!" His voice rang with excitement. "It's not Downeast. It's Mid Coast, but look at it! The lake is right there, and the seacoast is just a few miles east. It's priced at less than half of what it would take for us to build from scratch, not to mention the time factor. I was looking for cottages. I thought, why not this place? I can put the studio right there." He directed my eyes to an interior photo.

I hesitated.

"You mean, set aside the Downeast property and buy this instead?"

"Yes! It's in a great area for art and a better area for jobs."

"What will we do with the Downeast place, then?"

There was a pregnant pause.

"We'll figure it out." Optimist's code for "I have absolutely no idea".

Within minutes, we'd lobbed an email to the realtor and called my brother, a Mainer, who agreed to go look at the place for us. In typical fashion, by Saturday morning, we'd made an offer subject to further inspections and title work.

"Another house purchase over the internet. This is becoming a habit," I marveled aloud at our own daring.

We didn't share our unconventional buying method with everyone. The Council of Four took our eccentricity in stride and joined in our excitement. When the house inspection reports came in with favorable results, I felt the hairs stand up on my neck.

On a sunny Omaha day in mid-April, we walked into the title company's office and, ten minutes later, left it, marveling at how uncomplicated a house closing could be without a bank or lawyer involved. We now had two properties, a home and a piece of land in Maine. Peter squeezed my hand.

"It's only two months since my piano prophesy," I observed,

wonder-stricken. Even I had not fully taken my prediction seriously.

"I thought about that, too," he said. "Eerie."

That night after work, we arranged to fly out to see our new home for the first time. With our destination settled, there was just one more problem to solve: employment. The art market was still depressed, and as we'd concluded the hot dog stand was not a fit, a regular job was our only option. Peter, the great Job Whisperer, kicked into high gear on this front for both him and for me, despite my vehement objections for him.

"We have to keep all options on the table," he said, effectively censuring my disapproval. "We may have to take this in stages. If I have to take a job, we'll just sort things out differently once we get there."

When we needed his feet on the ground, the artist knew how to land.

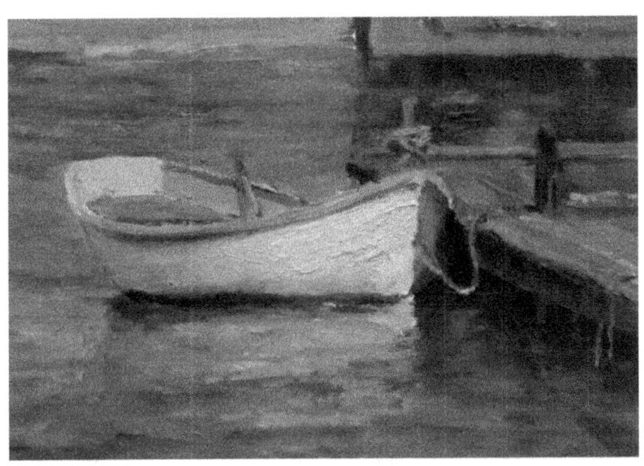

27

Supporting the Arts

"Without art, the crudeness of reality would make the world unbearable."
—George Bernard Shaw

We flew into Bangor and used GPS to find our way to the new house on a gorgeous spring afternoon. The long driveway was lined with brush and trees budded with pale green promise.

"This is like unwrapping a gift," I remarked to Peter as we stepped across the front door threshold.

The structure was pretty much what we'd understood from afar, sound and inhabitable but unfinished and needing some cosmetic TLC. We were immensely satisfied with our decision and particularly the fact that we would not be building from scratch, so that art would not have to take a back seat during a protracted construction phase. Peter showed me the soon-to-be studio.

"It's too small!" I declared, dropping my shoulders in dismay.

"It's bigger than what I have now!" laughed Peter, waving aside my concern.

"True," I conceded, "but your new work, the new seascape,

Incoming, and the paintings of the Northwoods…these are large canvases."

"We'll manage," he assured me.

Just prior to our trip, Peter had met me at the garage door a second time.

"What now?" I'd asked curiously.

"I've found a job in Maine," he'd told me, casting a sideways glance at me that left me a bit apprehensive.

We'd both climbed the basement stairs and walked into the living room to the computer, where a job listing was enlarged on the screen. I'd read it and immediately balked.

"This is what I'm doing now!" I'd cried, "I need a change. I want less pressure."

"I know this isn't what you want," he had answered gently, "really, I do. But once I found the ad, I felt I couldn't hide it. That would be making a decision for you instead of letting you decide. Even if you do apply, it may come to nothing and, anyway, if you don't like it, you can always say no."

The pragmatic and creative voices inside me had instantly gone head-to-head in fierce battle. My own desire for a change warred with the knowledge that my commitment to Peter had not yet been fulfilled and my deep belief that he deserved the chance to finish what he'd started. My hope for a less demanding job, I also knew, flew in the face of our financial needs of the moment. It was all so circular and so confused in my head, that, in the end, not sure of what to do, I decided to buy time by keeping my hat in the ring and sent in my resume. *At least,* I'd reasoned stoically to myself, *if I had to do the same work, we'd finally be in Maine. We'd be that much closer to the dream.* After all, no job had to be forever. One step and one metamorphosis at a time.

Despite the lingering economic depression in Maine, it didn't take long for the job applications to bear fruit. In the two weeks after our visit to the Mid Coast house, I made two more round trips to Maine for in-person interviews and set up three Skype interviews. For a clean background, we used the sunroom for Skyping, blocking off what sunlight we could for the late spring days.

On the day of one of my interviews, I drained a huge glass of water against the heat, spread out my notes and waited for the incoming call. There I sat, dressed in a suit from the waist up, excess network cable curled up at my feet and curtains taped closed, hoping the neighbor's overactive dogs would stay quiet just long enough.

The midday sun pounded the room, giving me an unusually rosy complexion that was probably interpreted as nervousness. I just prayed they didn't think I'd been drinking, though the thought of a chilled glass of wine was very appealing at the moment. Peter had drilled me beforehand so I would have my thoughts together and avoid being tongue-tied. Had he not, I was sure that faltering speech in combination with my flushed face would have sent up red flags to any prospective employer. Looking straight into the camera as rehearsed, I answered the call and began.

The whirlwind of job interviews left me exhausted in body and in spirit. Several offers arrived, although not one for the kind of job change I craved. Peter's search for himself yielded a few interviews but no offers. *The cards are played*, I admitted to myself, and I accepted the very job I'd initially rejected out of hand. It was a bittersweet moment, and I pushed through the disappointment by keeping the primary goal in mind: to jumpstart Peter's art career in the right market.

"This will get us there and get you on the right road with your painting," I told Peter, steeling myself to reality. "I'll deal with the rest after we're settled." I could not even entertain another five-year plan. "Let's give it a few years," I committed to the artist, "then we'll see. Maybe it'll surprise me."

The sobering truth was that our new life, like the old, would involve long hours doing the same thing I'd been doing for years plus a fairly long commute to work every day. Steeling myself to my lot, I didn't just set my writing aside; I put it in hibernation. There would be no room for it in the foreseeable future and no point trying to split myself down the middle pretending it could be so. Still, with a little work, I managed to find compensations.

"I love beginnings," I told Peter as we shifted into high gear for the second move in twelve months. "And living in the exhilarating beauty of Maine and watching you paint out there among other New England artists will be food for my soul."

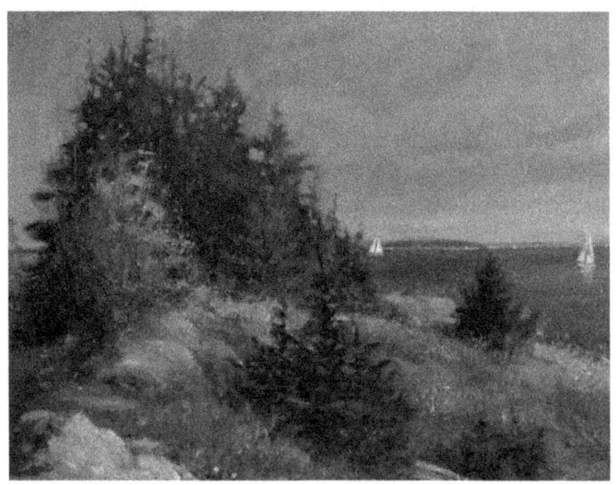

28

Art in Transit

*"An object in motion tends to remain in motion along a straight line
unless acted upon by an outside force."*
—Isaac Newton

Before we knew it, it was moving day. When we woke up that
morning in late July, the artist in Peter was unrecognizable; he became
a machine.

"What do you mean there's no truck?" he demanded, the pitch
of his voice uncharacteristically high.

It was seven o'clock in the morning, and the moving truck and
car trailer he'd ordered were not at the lot. The service person made
several calls, then returned to inform us that the truck was on its way
from another Omaha location. Our accelerated respiration slowed.

"Well, if that's the only glitch in the proceedings," I said lightly,
"we'll be heading east in no time."

I left Peter at the truck depot and went to the office for the last
time.

Around one thirty, the summer heat having reached 95 degrees

(110 inside the truck), I arrived home with lunch and to assist with packing. It became quickly clear that the final packing was a long way off.

"Good thing we ordered the larger truck and got rid of so much," I said, frowning concernedly at the crammed contents.

"Yeah," Peter grunted, sweat pouring off his face and soaking his shirt.

The two movers we'd hired to help didn't look much better. I scanned the contents of the garage where all the remaining stuff had been staged to facilitate packing, and my heart sank.

"Peter," I called, waving him over, "all of this isn't going to fit in that truck."

He'd been so busy inside the truck that he'd lost track of the overall picture. The culprit, in my estimation, was the volume of boxes, which I put down to "art creep", Peter's continually but imperceptibly expanding studio contents.

After donations to our neighbor, negotiations with the two hired movers to take what they wanted, and a final trip to Goodwill, the last items were finally loaded: our box spring and mattress (so they'd be the first to come off) and the well-crated *Crescendo* painting. In a fit of efficiency, Peter had devised a plan to stop at the gallery on the way to our new house to deliver the work. I cringed as I watched him cram that boxed painting into a vertical position at the back of the truck.

"What if everything shifts? It'll get crushed," I worried.

"No chance," he answered confidently, carefully lowering the moving truck door. "It's a strong box, and there's not a quarter of an inch to spare in there. Nothing will move."

"Until you open the door again," I predicted. "We'll have to be ready to catch whatever falls."

The final step, loading the hatchback onto the trailer, took over two hours because we'd been given the wrong size trailer and had to wait for a replacement. The collective effect of all the delays meant we were not underway until eight thirty at night, Tasha tucked snugly between us on the seat.

"Three hours to Des Moines. Maybe we should get a room right here in Omaha," I suggested.

"No," answered Peter wearily through gritted teeth. "After all this work, I need to feel like we've actually left."

We fell onto the motel mattress around one o'clock in the morning, the slow-moving diesel having lengthened our travel time. By four thirty, we were heading east again. Normally, I would have driven while Peter napped and vice versa so that we shared the load. I, however, had no experience handling a 26-foot truck at highway speeds with a trailer dragging behind, so Peter had undertaken to do all the driving.

The reality of this arrangement was much more difficult than we'd imagined. The diesel engine was so loud that the audio books and music we'd planned to ease the time and keep the driver alert were out of the question. Talking, except in short, loud bursts, was impossible. By noon, the temperature reached the upper 90's and, due to the hillier terrain, we had to turn off the air conditioning to give the diesel engine enough power for the inclines. At our lunch stop, we had to sneak Tasha into the restaurant just to cool her down.

Our next stop was in Indiana.

"We'll arrive a bit late but should have a good night's rest," I assured my weary chauffeur.

This would have been true had our GPS been able to properly locate the motel. We didn't find it until close to midnight but were nevertheless back on the road again by four thirty to beat the morning traffic.

I called ahead to our final overnight stop in Albany, New York to make sure the motel would accept the moving truck and dog.

"Yes," answered the motel clerk unequivocally.

At check-in, the clerk was of a different mindset and told us to "find somewhere else to park". Peter stubbornly pulled in, stretching the truck across parking spaces at the back of the lot, then instantly walked the grounds to check our exit so we'd be prepared in the morning. In the meantime, I tentatively settled into the revolting motel room, the kind where you don't want to remove your shoes for fear of what's in the carpeting, let alone use the bed or bathroom. It took all my attention to subdue Tasha's agitation at the dogs barking incessantly from other rooms. I called the clerk to appeal for quiet.

We ordered a pizza—extra large, extra cheese, extra vegetables, extra everything—and downed the whole thing in record time while sitting on the edge of the grungy bed in a fit of worry. Peter's search of the grounds had revealed that the exit path was comprised of hairpin turns and littered with parked cars, making it impossible for the truck and trailer to pass.

"We're going to have to back out the entrance, and it's uphill," he warned.

This prospect alone was enough to keep us both awake, but latecomers kept swinging in to park in the truck's exit path so Peter had to repeatedly step out to negotiate their relocation. Still on driveway watch at three o'clock, he said finally, "Let's just go. I'd rather be moving than sitting here enduring this."

I compliantly packed up the few items we'd exposed to the repulsive room and marched up to my assigned position near the exit. Peter climbed into the driver's seat, Tasha at his side, ear pieces jammed tightly into his ears to hear my directions by cell phone over the roar of the diesel. I had to yell, which drew the motel clerk and a number of guests to the lobby window to watch the proceedings. Ignoring them, I guided Peter inch by inch backwards up the long drive, past the cars in the packed lot, around the portico roof and out onto the road. Then, I quickly hopped into the passenger seat. A car behind us pounded the horn in protest of the 60 seconds we'd blocked the road. It was a sendoff fitted to the place, noisy and crude.

With no sleep, no breakfast, not even a sip of coffee, we rolled onto the MassPike to face the slopes through The Berkshires at fifteen to twenty miles per hour, the fastest the packed diesel could travel uphill, the uncomfortable remains of more pizza than two people should ever eat sitting in our stomachs. It took a while for our optimism to rise to the surface, but it came out with the morning sun.

"Our next stop is Maine," I reminded Peter meaningfully, as rays of light sprayed across the sky in front of us.

It was enough. We had survived the night unscathed—no bedbugs, belongings intact—and had narrowly escaped the motel parking lot. We felt all the good fortune of it.

Dirty and sweaty, we'd had seven hours of restless sleep in three days. Our eyes were bloodshot and darkly circled, and the truck seat smelled like dog. Despite my continuous brushing and shaking out of blankets, dog hairs floated everywhere in the sunlit cab, sending us into sneezing fits and settling all over our clothing. Even with the engine off, we spoke to one another in raised voices, having become half deafened by the truck.

Pouring some rest stop coffee down my throat to stiffen my resolve, I asked, "What's next?"

"Once we cross into Maine," Peter yelled, "we'll pull over and call the gallery about truck clearance. I don't want to get this thing stuck on a back street just trying to deliver a painting."

By late morning, we crossed the Maine border. "Welcome to Maine: the way life should be", the sign read. Peter laughed a bit nervously, I thought, but I broke into sobs. How many obstacles had we cleared just over the last three days let alone the last three years to get past that state line? We were finally here, although fully cognizant that "here" is a relative term in The Pine Tree State. The house would still be three hours away (four to five in diesel truck time) after the gallery drop off.

I helped Peter navigate off the highway into the little coastal town where the gallery would exhibit the *Crescendo* painting. He pulled safely into a school parking lot with a clear and easy exit path while I dialed the gallery.

"Hi," I said, "We're in a 26-foot truck with a trailer attached less than a mile from the gallery. Is there any way someone could meet us so we don't have to risk getting stuck on the side road? It's hard to maneuver."

"No."

I mouthed the answer to Peter.

"OK, then, how close can we get to the gallery in a truck this size?"

"You can pull right up," the gallery worker assured me. "We have big trucks come through here all the time."

I thanked her dubiously and hung up.

We rolled watchfully forward, avoiding darting pedestrians as we searched for the gallery's street. There it was, a narrow one-way lane that required a sharp left turn and had no room to swing wide. Peter rolled his eyes and continued up the shoreline road until he found space to pull over. Then, he sunk his head down onto the steering wheel and let out a huge sigh. I wanted to encourage him with "We're almost there", but we hadn't yet opened the back of the truck, and judging from the experience we'd had so far, the assumption that we had a painting to deliver was, in my estimation, a tad over-confident.

Slipping out our respective doors, we both stepped to the back, unlocked the truck door and inched it upward, bracing to catch the fallout. None came. Peter deftly removed the boxed painting and reclosed the truck door.

"No puncture holes," he exclaimed happily, examining the box. He opened it and smiled. "All right and tight. I'll be back shortly."

Grimy, disheveled and covered in dog hair as he was, exhausted in body and soul, he popped that four-by-six-foot box atop his head and began the half mile walk back the other way to introduce himself and his work to a new gallery while Tasha and I waited in the hot truck.

On his return, Peter reported, "There was no way this truck would have got in there…or out."

Still, the deed was done. We grinned at one another. It's not that the mishaps of the last few days were forgotten. It's just that this single hard-won achievement, a seascape painting delivered to a seacoast gallery in Maine, reminded us why we'd endured all this.

We headed back out onto the highway with renewed spirit. Several hours later, we pulled off the interstate onto Route 3. This two-lane highway is an experience in the warping of time. The road sign says fifty miles to Belfast, but it feels more like one hundred-fifty, and that's before converting to diesel miles. After an eternity, we hit Belfast, rolled across the Passagassawakeag bridge and swung a wide left onto Route 141 toward Swanville Lake. When we passed the little grocery by the lake dam, our morale lifted. This was the home stretch.

The truck finally pulled to a squealing stop in front of the house. We spilled out, sucking in the fresh pine air and no longer repressing our aversion to the pungent cab. Peter lifted Tasha to the ground and ordered, "Go explore." She didn't need prodding.

Stepping inside the house, dirty, smelly, still talking loudly and shaking from the vibrations of the road, we let the transformation begin. We were home with all the significance of the move yet to transpire. We walked through each room to rediscover the place, then emptied and unloaded the car from the trailer and raced down to the little grocery for some provisions. The last task of the day before a hot shower was to pull the mattress from the back of the truck, last to load, first to be removed, one of the few things about this move that went as planned.

"Welcome to Maine," I whispered to Peter before closing my eyes and thinking no more.

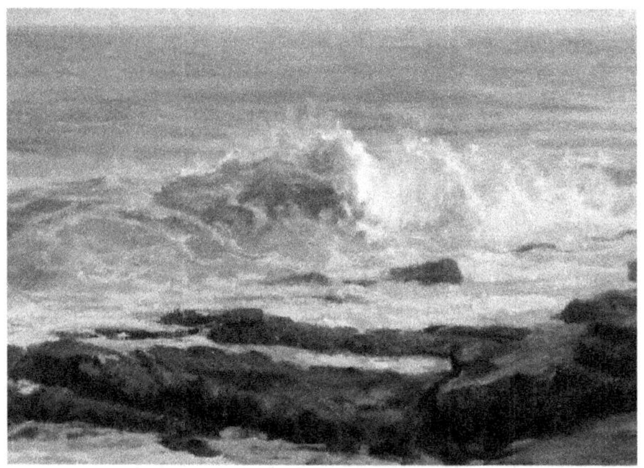

29

Watercolor

"I will do water—beautiful, blue water."
—Claude Monet

This was the first home we'd purchased with the full intention from day one that Peter was an established, professional artist. Next to living essentials, the artist's workspace was our top priority, but setting up the studio was easier said than done. The room had been designed to be a commodious entrance, not an actual room. It was dark, small and further constricted by three doorways on one end. The house had no basement, nor any garage, for spillover storage. The accumulated art creep now lay before us in its full extreme and had to be crammed into the back of the room in piles that reached the ceiling. If Peter had any kind of ego, which he did not, it would be kept in check by this fraction of a real studio.

"Why is all this other junk in here?" I asked, surveying the non-art-related boxes compounding the space problem.

"This stuff can't be left out in the weather," he explained matter-of-factly. "There's no place else to put it until the garage is

141

built." He reassured me optimistically, "I've already got more space than I had in the rental. And I'll be painting outside in this weather anyway."

I wasn't sure how to interpret Peter's reaction to the new studio. Stoicism? Exhaustion? The flexibility provision? Eyeing the confined corner where he'd gamely made a spot for his easel, I made a mental comparison to the spacious studios graced with character, vaulted ceilings, and even breath-taking views, that he'd admired in the past. These great rooms were more in keeping with what I'd envisioned for him by this point in his art travels.

I suspected, though, that I would never hear a peep from the painter. He would toil wordlessly in his crammed studio ever conscious that I had taken on the less appealing task of working in an office day after day to make it possible. *It will be up to me*, I realized, *to initiate improvements in here. Peter will never raise a single complaint.* I made a quick list in my head, starting with a coat of neutral paint as soon as the junk was cleared, and pressed Peter to find a garage contractor as quickly as possible.

Just five days after we'd fallen out of the smelly truck onto Maine soil, house in a state of utter confusion, and well before I'd caught up on lost sleep, I stepped into the office of my new employer. Despite my preparations the night before, the morning had been a scramble. Our disorganized bedroom, poorly lit and painted a deep purple by the former owners, cast shadows on my morning ritual. Worse, the wall color combined with the butterfly border paper recalled to me some Lunesta sleeping pill commercials, leaving me loopy and a little nauseated.

"I know painting the bedroom is the least of our concerns right now," I said as I shoved down the meager breakfast my nervous stomach would tolerate, "but that purple and butterfly combo has got to go." The "Lunesta Room" was placed at the top of the painting list after the studio, though only God knew when we'd get to it.

Peter kissed me good-bye, then, boxes be damned, jumped right into the Maine art world like he was on fire. It wasn't hard to identify his focal point. Water, water was everywhere and on every canvas he brought home. He just couldn't get enough, as if we'd been living in the desert for the last decade. From his perspective, I guess we had.

Throughout the coming weeks, my phone buzzed on my desk to announce incoming photos of breath-taking water views, Peter's way of sharing the beauty with his office-bound partner.

"There's so much material! I can't stop taking photos," Peter told me, laughing at himself, "as if I'm still a tourist. It's going to take time to register that I actually live here now."

"Don't stop!" I begged. "I love it."

I eagerly awaited all the beauty he could send my way, a lifeline connecting my daily grind to the venture it was supporting.

I took in snippets of Maine when I could. There was a nest of eagles on the building where I worked, and the birds soared gracefully in the air at the closest distance I'd ever been to their kind. I grabbed the few stimulating glimpses of blue water I could get along the way to work while the morning light lasted. For the time being, I settled for experiencing Maine vicariously through Peter.

It became quickly and abundantly clear that the work I needed to accomplish at my new job was nothing short of crushing, so my focus narrowed to this task. I worked seven days a week, usually twelve to fourteen hours per day. In between, I slept and ate and grabbed what time I could to organize the house, which I could measure more in minutes than hours. Living, truly living, in Maine was confined to short clips. Working was my reality. Watching Peter grow was just about all the attention I could spare and, fortunately, all the gratification I needed for the moment.

Before I knew it, I was rolling into a completed garage and stepping through the door to a newly painted studio which, now clear of junk, exhibited as much of Peter's new work as the limited wall space could hold. He had painted so prolifically en plein air in the few months since our arrival that he'd already run out of hanging space, a far cry from his constrained outdoor work in the Midwest Plains.

"Let's use the hallway," I suggested, waving my arm at the long empty walls running through the center of the house. "We'll call it the 'Great Gallery'." It, too, was filled it in no time. "I love being surrounded by your work," I told him admiringly, "but you need outlets, real galleries."

He turned to me excitedly.

"I just got into an exhibit in Boothbay, and I'm already knocking on gallery doors."

The man was ablaze with motivation.

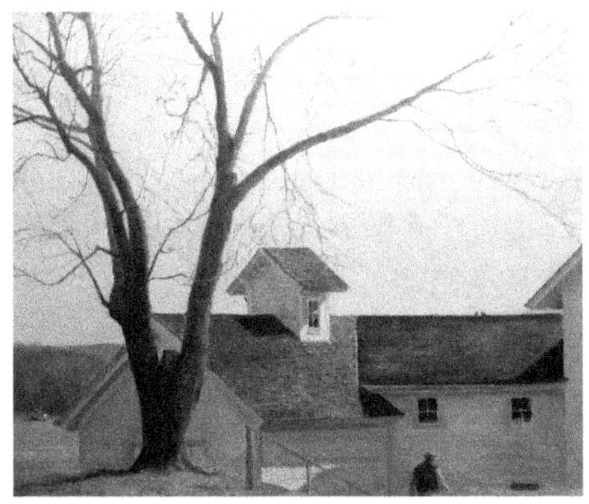

30

The Art of Gratitude

"The essence of all beautiful art, all great art, is gratitude."
—Friedrich Nietzsche

"What's that on the canvas there?" I asked, leaning in to look more closely at Peter's seascape of the day.

"Oh, those are gnats," he said, rolling his eyes and sweeping his fingers across the buggy spot. Plein air painting has its challenges.

I noted with astonishment the progress in his seascapes already evident in his burgeoning work. The rapidity and fearlessness with which he'd taken to painting Maine were incredible. And he had jumped right into the art community, agreeing to host the Plein Air Painters of Maine Northern Chapter and excitedly seeking out and posting painting locations each week where artists could converge to paint.

"Only a few have shown up so far," he told me without the smallest hint of discouragement. "I'm mostly on my own. I don't mind, as long as I can be out there."

His gaze automatically shifted to the window as he spoke the last two words.

Amidst this breakneck artistic expansion, there emerged an unanticipated crisis that could have derailed everything in these early days. I needed to vent the pressures of my job, which were great, but, when I did so, Peter transmuted my venting into guilt. His knee-jerk reaction was to declare that he should get a job so I could rest.

"You look so tired, and I feel bad that there's no end in sight," he lamented.

"Me, too," I answered honestly, "but that was our deal. I need to know you can let me offload without feeling the only solution is to change places." I looked at him entreatingly. "Don't think of rescuing me; think of supporting me. And keep up your art. That's what I'm working for."

Already the best listener I knew, Peter became an exemplary counselor with just the right degree of detachment. He was helped by a new and now dear art friend, who advised him, "Accept her gift so you can, in turn, give your gift of art to the world", advice, I believe, that brought him to the tipping point.

And true to our partnership, he worked harder at his art than I'd ever seen. Each night after supper, as I sat down at the computer to resume office work, he would announce, "If you work, I work," and head straight back to the studio where he painted until I logged off. I felt gratified that, in spite of the pressures of work and the hours we spent apart, our rhythms were still synchronized.

Where Peter found the time and energy to paint so productively and keep the home fires burning as he did was a mystery to me. He used good weather days to paint and also to start garden beds, build compost bins, and rough out a dog pen.

"Big pile," I observed, eyeing the gigantean mountain of flattened boxes at the back of the house as we surveyed the progress one weekend.

"Lots of garden beds," he rejoined without hesitation, grinning and rubbing his hands together.

He had researched permaculture gardening and devised a great recycling scheme to use all the moving paper and boxes as the bottom layer of our new beds. I guessed this was where all the art-creep boxes were finally going to pay off.

I took heart in all the progress at home and found novel ways to keep my hand in art. My office became a revolving art gallery—"Gallery North", we called it—a way to immerse myself in the newest work until it was delivered to a real gallery. From time to time, I'd find views in my business travels for Peter to paint: a field of lupine blooms, an old stone building, a magnificent vista. One morning, not two miles from home, I pulled the car over to the side of the road and called him from my cell phone.

"Get up here right away," I urged excitedly. "The morning sun is just coming up over the hills and it's exquisite."

Then, I hopped back in my car and took off for work, looking forward to show-and-tell over dinner.

With all this, every single day, supper was ready to serve when I arrived home. Candles were lit, soft music was playing, and wine was poured, all meant to enhance the limited time I could devote to relaxation.

"Welcome home," Peter greeted me one night, giving me an odd look as I hung up my coat.

"Thanks."

I openly sighed my relief to be there and turned toward the Lunesta Room for my usual change out of stiff office attire into soft, comfortable flannels. *Wait.* I stopped abruptly in the bedroom doorway, then spun around to find Peter standing right behind me wearing a monstrous grin. In a single day, he had removed the syrupy butterfly border paper and painted a white primer over the oppressive dark purple. Just as we entered the darkest days of the year, we had light. It had taken all his self-control to let me discover the surprise myself.

Maine slid into an early winter. Peter cobbled together some winter gear and kept right on painting at all his announced spots, usually the sole artist braving the elements. Maine en plein air was like a drug, and he was its most unapologetic new addict.

"Where did you get all this stuff?" I asked him, staring at a big pile of clothing on the couch when I got home.

"I'm freezing out there," he explained. "I went to Goodwill

and bought a bunch of warm clothes. I'm going to get paint all over them anyway, so there's no point in buying new."

He looked like a walking rummage sale. No matter. He was warm. He was painting. And the only beauty that interested Peter was what he put on his canvases.

We were both uncertain of our new ground and more comfortable with our agile year-by-year planning in place of our usual five-year scheme. In the moments we had to talk, Peter laid out thoughts about his work for the coming year.

"This is a big state. I'm still learning where to go to paint, meet artists and find galleries," he said as I helped him nail mounting strips to the studio walls and create more hanging space in the Great Gallery. "I have to get my bearings and make my work representative of Maine. I need to understand Maine's unique market. It's different from other areas, even along the East Coast."

The artist had a steep hill to climb to establish himself in a new region from the ground up, factoring in the effects of the Great Recession as well.

"That's a full plate," I observed.

"No fuller than yours," he said gently, pulling me into a hug.

Regardless of his own pressures, every morning, Peter joined me for breakfast in the wee hours, made my lunch and walked me to the car as I had once done for him. Between decreasing daylight and long work hours, I left and returned in the dark, so I eagerly awaited the unveiling of the improvements each weekend in the light of day. I pulled away in the pitch dark repeating my mantra of gratitude for Peter, for all that was opening up to him, and for my job, which was making it all possible.

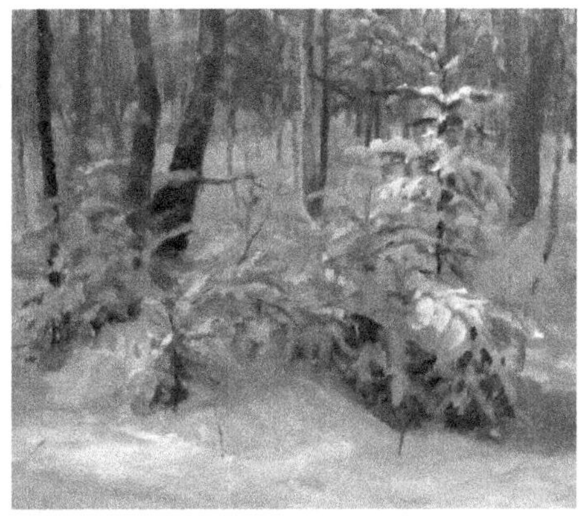

31

Freezing Paint

As if Maine expressly designed our first winter to test newcomers "from away", it snowed regularly from Election Day to April. Even the natives complained. By late winter, the freeze had overcome the back roads, buckling them in ripples that challenged the struts. The snow on the driveway had compacted into six inches of solid ice which we navigated with ice cleats. The accumulated snow that had slid from our roof grew taller than the windows, blocking the warm southern sunlight that normally streamed into our living room. We'd raked the heavier snowfalls from the roof by climbing the snow piles in our new snow shoes. Birds flocked to our feeders, and wild turkeys gathered underneath to take advantage of fallen seeds.

From my regular vantage point, the office window, I could see gorgeous white ice formations on the river that, when struck by the winter sun, bore lights and shadows of yellows and blues. We couldn't help but wonder what the spring melt would bring, though it was clear that ice jams and flooding were definitely on the menu.

Peter's painting never missed a beat during the winter extremities, though when the water views morphed from slate blue to choppy ice floes, he turned inland. He was painting larger and better than ever en plein air, despite the weather. The dauntless artist discovered gloves with open fingertips for freedom of dexterity, but by the time the subzero temperatures hit, these were displaced by hand-warming charcoal packets stuffed into old socks. His Goodwill wardrobe was insulating him well. He also recovered an old one-piece snowsuit from the garage and learned the value of a very large thermos of hot tea.

"You need to protect your face," I said, reaching over with a pained expression and smearing petroleum jelly over his raw, red cheeks as we had done when we were kids. He squirmed a bit but couldn't argue with its effectiveness against the chafing cold and wind. Deep snow and high wind slowed Peter down a bit, but he was hardy in the cold and came home only when the temperature overtook his palette, thickening the paint and stiffening the brushes.

I'd never before associated artists with athletes, but the plein air artist is in a separate class. Hauling art gear through snow in heavy boots and winter insulation, then standing in the bitter cold for hours, is a feat of both strength and endurance.

"You're going to have to work to maintain your stamina out there," I coached Peter, "if you want to remain fit for plein air painting throughout the year."

"I know, I know," he answered without enthusiasm.

Since he'd left high school wrestling behind, Peter had struggled with the discipline of regular exercise. Now, it was essential to his work. I came home one night to find him in the middle of the living room grinding and sweating in concert with one of his exercise DVDs. I grinned. He didn't.

He spent most of his time painting alone that winter.

"I wish more artists would go out with you," I said. "Doesn't it get kind of lonely?"

"No," he answered unhesitatingly. "I'm so enthralled by what I'm painting, I don't even notice I'm by myself. And Tasha comes with me."

Regardless of temperature, our fluffy white terrier sprightly hopped into the truck, tail wagging and body frissoning *Road trip!* every time Peter left for a plein air painting excursion. Even as the weather turned cold, she remained his loyal companion, though her job on frigid days was to wait patiently in the warm cab while the artist worked. Feeling left out, she began a whining campaign to be by Peter's side that she could sustain for hours. Plagued by her incessant complaining, he let her out and attempted to keep her by his side on a leash. Tasha shivered, paced, fidgeted and finally wrapped the leash around his legs and easel, nearly toppling the painting.

"I can't take her with me anymore," he announced sadly, throwing up his hands. "She's just too high maintenance."

So much for the idyllic image of artist and devoted dog.

Aside from plein air attempts and snow removal, winter was otherwise a quiet season, giving Peter a chance to catch up in the studio and on extraneous matters like sourcing better frames and researching galleries. Often, we'd spend the dinner hour reviewing his findings.

"What do you think of these?" he asked, spreading a bag of frame samples across the kitchen table and then grabbing one at a time to model against the corner of a new painting. This was an exercise in visualization with no guarantee of a favorable result, as was evidenced by the growing stack of disappointing frames accumulating in the storage closet. "I wish we could find a better way than trial and error," said Peter, discouraged, as he added another rejected frame to the pile.

"It's just one of those learning curves," I answered. "We'll get it narrowed down eventually."

Just as the long hard winter became unendurable, spring did come. The sun shone. The ice melted. The roads unbuckled. Peter found the Castine lighthouse and Blue Hill.

At the first opportunity afforded by the weather, he finished the dog pen he'd begun in the fall using green fencing wire over a wood frame with a little wooden house for shelter. On her inaugural day in the new pen, Tasha bent and chewed the wire with her teeth until she created a hole large enough to escape. Peter returned home to find her basking in the sun on the front stoop.

I looked down at her tiny snout.

"Does she transform while we're gone?" my eyes widened as we examined the damage. I had visions of Milo, the Jack Russell terrier in the movie *The Mask*.

"Obviously," answered Peter grittily, as he grabbed a sheet of paper and began to sketch new plans for a solid wooden pen. "I can get free wood pallets from the dump."

He looked over at me in his ever-vigilant spirit of economy, not wanting to waste a single penny I earned. Besides, there was no point investing in new wood without certainty it would survive the first trial.

One sunny weekend, I took a rare break from office work and drove with Peter to Stonington.

"I can't wait to show you this cove," he said excitedly. "I've named it for you, well, in my mind, at least," he added. "I'm sure it already has a name. It's just that every time I look at it, I can't help thinking of you. It has all the things you love about the coast."

He was right. It was perfect. I felt the sea air on my face, put my toes in the icy, lapping water and inhaled the pine and salt scents. Bright as the moment was, it made me conscious that my energy was alarmingly low. It had been hard to dismiss, in the past few months, the growing concern reflected on Peter's face and on the faces of friends and family for my health and well-being. In this quiet moment at the cove, I felt acutely what they had been seeing.

"You can quit whenever you've had enough," Peter had insisted time and again. "We'll work it out".

I'd held out, wanting to give him more time for his art venture and maintaining that the hours and fatigue were normal for the early months of a responsible job.

"You'll see," I'd told him. "Six months in, it'll begin to calm down. I just have to get through until then. I can do it."

By now, nine months had passed and, contrary to my prediction, work continued at the same volume and rate of pressure, seven days a week. Despite the sunlit day, I felt a different kind of cold running up my back.

Dusk began to shadow the cove, so we reluctantly packed up and headed for home, looking for signs of spring along the way. Peter's eyes were still searching for buds and birds as he turned into the driveway.

"Oh, no," was all he said, bringing the car to a premature standstill. There on the front stoop lay Tasha. She'd torn apart the wood planks of her new pen, then squeezed through the splintered hole. Still bleeding from her escape, she proudly stood up, tongue extended, tail wagging at the sight of us.

"She has the jaws of a Rottweiler," I said, looking incredulously at the mangled pen. Tasha the Terrible had thrown down the gauntlet, but I could see from Peter's eyes that the days of her reign of terror were numbered.

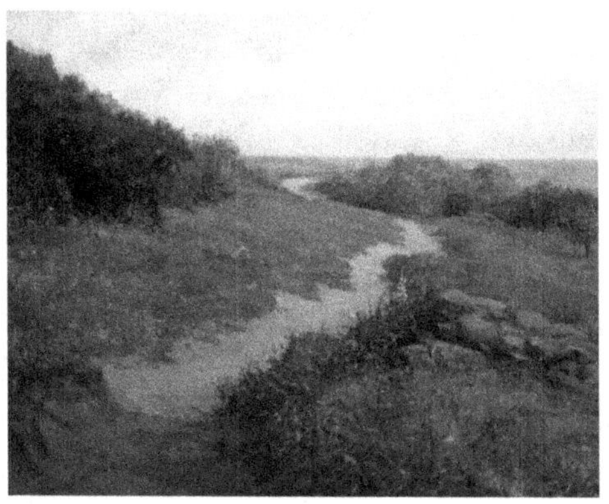

32

Al Fresco

"Nothing makes me so happy as to observe nature and to paint what I see."
—Henri Rousseau

As the weather warmed, Maine came alive in a dramatic burst, and the population mushroomed with tourists. Calls began to roll in from friends and family who wanted to see our new place and take in a bit of Maine in the season.

"Our house was infinitely superior in Omaha but was never such a draw," I laughed.

No matter. Peter and I loved visitors. By now, he was familiar with many painting hot spots along the coast—islands, light houses, boat yards and beaches. He delighted in the idea of taking our guests to Maine's iconic locations as well as to more isolated spots of particular beauty. He could manage a good deal of painting around our company while they hiked, swam and picnicked. I joined them when I could.

Reserving the early and late hours of dramatic daylight for plein air painting, Peter used the in-between hours for gardening, as always, with one eye on me.

"I know you love it," he said, spreading wheelbarrow after wheelbarrow of topsoil and wood chips across the permaculture beds. "You regroup when your hands are in the dirt. I want you to have that."

I wanted it, too, though I wasn't sure how I would find the time.

"The work should be letting up by now," I fretted, turning from the computer to face Peter. "I just can't catch my breath. I have no time to reflect. I just jump from task to task and back again. There's so much work. How will I ever help with the garden?" I felt a constrictive panic grip my chest.

"It's not an obligation," he reassured me. "The garden will be here whenever you want it for the time you have." What a guy.

Gardening itch and longer days meant seedlings, and lots of them. Normally, I was the one who started the planting, always in numbers carefully calculated to serve our needs. Peter took on the baby project that year and, true to his nature, his method was more freeform and expansive. For lack of a better location, he began to lay out flats and pots in front of the sliding glass doors of our combination kitchen-dining-living-great room. Before long, large swaths of the floor were overtaken by seedlings underway, curtailing other activities. I insisted on a lighted shelf unit to take advantage of vertical space. It made little difference. He just found more pots.

"I feel like they're breeding when our backs our turned. Do you think we should rent a room until they all leave home?" I asked sarcastically, gingerly stepping around flats to get to the couch. When Peter got creative, it was hard to hold back the tide.

At his rate of industry, I needn't have worried about the seedlings; they were all in the ground before the guests started arriving. Among the first that season were our son and daughter-in-law, still active and immensely helpful in the Council of Four. Their housewarming gift, our first ever lobster pot, clearly stated their priorities and dictated the menu for the next night.

After an invigorating trip to Acadia National Park, we scooped up some salt water in the cooler, picked up lobsters and headed home for a feast. As I delivered the steaming orange beauties to their respective cobalt blue plates, I was struck by the bold colors. There had been a time when Peter would have hopped up to capture the moment for a still life. Not now. His concentration was all for marine and landscape painting, his strong still life skills shelved for a new era with new priorities. As I watched him tend the fire pit after our lobsterfest, there was no mistake that his fit to the Maine outdoors was hand-in-glove. In our backyard, on the trails, at the waterside, no matter where, his alignment of spirit with the place was obvious, and I thought it was showing in his work. Here was proof positive that our response to the irresistible draw of the coast had been the next natural step in his artistic progression.

Nebraska or Maine, speed was still Peter's demon. By this point, he was managing one nearly finished medium-sized canvas per day en plein air.

"You should see the other artists," he said, wringing his hands. "They paint two to three canvases—good sized ones—in a single day. I work so slowly that, with the light changing as often as it does, I end up repainting the same canvas without realizing it."

I listened to his frustration sympathetically. Surely, there were tricks to the trade, but at least a part of the difficulty came from nature. A thoughtful, paced personality with not a smidgeon of intensity, Peter had never been a person of exceptionally quick speed. Through sheer will and steady practice, he had nevertheless made remarkable gains.

"Look how far you've come," I pointed out, adding "Keep comparing yourself to your peers for inspiration but not to the point of self-defeat. You are not naturally fast. Keep score only against yourself and find your own level."

Watching him digest my words, I scrambled for something more tangible, aware as ever that my ideas often lagged behind Peter's own resourcefulness.

"Are you bringing enough canvases?" I asked. "If you tune into the light, and you have enough supplies to change out when it shifts, every one of them can be finished in the studio if needed."

He did just that.

With the longer summer days, Peter seized opportunities to introduce me to favorite local painting spots so I could experience first-hand what he had put on canvas.

"Quick! Get changed!" he urged me one evening, opening the car door as I came to a stop in the garage and grabbing my bags.

Exhausted though I was, I instantly obeyed, already peeling off my jacket as I quick-stepped to the door, sure that whatever he had planned had something to do with helping me relax. He quickly locked Tasha into her new and very sturdy, combination reinforced wire and wood pen and whisked me off to the brilliant blue bayside for some R & R with my supper. We ate leisurely on a park bench watching the light fade over the water.

"I don't want to leave," I said dismally as we began to pack up.

Who would cheerfully trade this vista for the sack full of work that awaited me at home? Nonetheless, home we went to resume the workday and to find Tasha once again curled up on the front stoop. The great fortress sported a giant hole where the unstoppable terrier jaws had again worked their evil. Tasha 3, Peter 0.

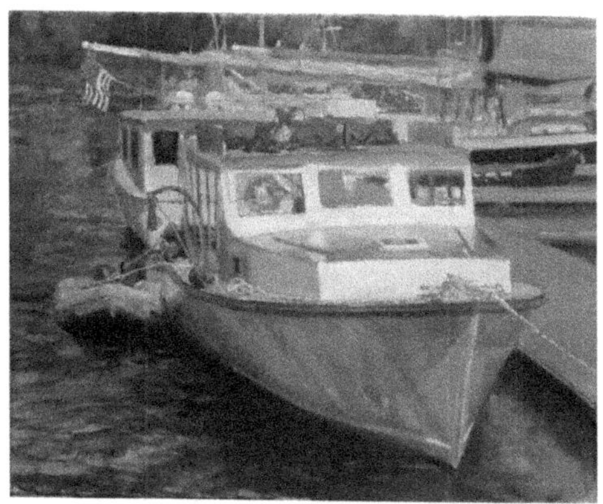

33

Art Gear

"Just let the wardrobe do the acting."
—Jack Nicholson

"Look at this."

Peter pointed to his knee where a terrible sunburn flamed in the exact shape of the slit in his paint-spattered jeans. If plein air painting was his future, he would have to dramatically amend his fashion statement.

"No more holes, no more baseball caps," I winced, eyeing his unnaturally red neck.

I envied him dressing within his comfort zone, but he had other wardrobe concerns. His fair complexion waged a constant battle with the summer sun, and the devious sunrays were unforgiving when he missed the minutest detail.

"You have a three-day event coming up," I cautioned, referring to his first juried plein air event in Maine. "You'd better have the right rig for the gig or you won't make it through the first day."

Later that week, I opened the door to find him in newly acquired pants from Goodwill and donning the wide-brimmed,

Monet-style hat he had bought after his first plein air class back in Omaha and now retrieved from the back of the supply closet.

"Total protection, head, neck and shoulders," he grinned at me proudly, turning comically to model the headgear.

"Looks, um, artsy," I said, a corner of my mouth involuntarily rising, "and there's certainly no chance of losing sight of you in that sombrero."

There should be a scout badge for plein air artists. They need to be armed against all the risks of the profession: temperature, sunburn, rain, dehydration, ticks, mosquitoes and so on.

"You're off to remote places and usually alone," I maintained, stuffing supplies into Peter's bag, "and your phone won't always work out there. It's best to be prepared."

Water. Protein. Sunscreen. Bug spray. Aspirin. First aid kit. Portable phone charger. Maps. Allergy medication. Peter complied without question, knowing well that any resistance would be countered by a repetition of the story of the angry bees who'd attacked him in remote country while he was painting. Peter is allergic, and disaster had been averted only because he'd had the proper medical kit, forced on him by She-Who-Must-Not-Be-Named, on hand to deal with the sting. The huge, wheeled back pack he'd found at Goodwill now bulged from every pocket with protective supplies. I'd never been a Girl Scout, but you don't have to actually wear the uniform if you were born with the gene.

Peter's makeover also extended to equipment. The traveling artist has a careful balance to maintain between the reliability and the portability of gear. He had assayed four easels thus far and had last settled on a professional pochade box on a tripod. This he now set aside for a newly homemade scrap wood pochade box and paint tray mounted on an old aluminum easel given to him by his aunt some years ago.

"What, no duct tape?" I asked him in a sardonic tone, recalling the last box he'd thrown together.

He threw me a look as he tied the huge, overloaded back pack to the underside of the lightweight tripod to demonstrate how it would serve double duty as an anchor against the wind. Then, piling all his gear onto his back to test the weight and balance, he asked, "How do I look?"

"Hobo and vagabond come to mind," I answered wryly.

I guessed it was a testament to our close partnership that Peter and I so often underwent change in tandem. Constrained for years by conservative dress codes, I'd collected a closet full of standard greys, blacks, navies and neutrals that I moderately accessorized with jewelry and scarves. Inspired by Peter's great wardrobe transformation, I was suddenly seized with the urge to allow my love of color freer expression. I started small but quickly cast aside all reserve and graduated to hot pink and cobalt blue shirts, red and purple sweaters and even a neon orange jacket that made everyone blink twice.

"I am an artist's wife, after all," I justified my purchases to Peter as I tossed a brilliant scarf over my shoulder. "I need to dress with a more interesting palette."

"I like this one," he complimented me as I plopped in the chair for breakfast in an emerald green jacket and a brightly polka-dotted scarf. I smiled in return. The butterfly had burst from its chrysalis and, in yet another way, I felt the warmth of synchronization with my partner.

The final preparation for the plein air event involved a different kind of transformation aimed at the overactive jaws of our little terrier. Once and for all, we needed a pen that could withstand her gnawing and prevent her from wandering while we were gone. In his travels, Peter spotted a six-foot tall chain-link dog pen laying in someone's front yard with a For Sale sign on it. He bought it on the spot and had it installed before I came home.

"She can't jump this one," he said, walking the perimeter and sizing up the arrangement. "She can't chew through the heavy metal. I've laid big rocks around the inner edge so she can't dig out."

Everything looked right and tight.

Next morning, I conducted a final scan of the vagabond's clothes for sunburn holes and, feeling that all contingencies were covered, pecked his cheek and sent him off well before daybreak. Just before I pulled out of the driveway, he was back.

"I forgot my brushes," he said sheepishly, then dashed off

again.

Sometimes, no amount of preparation is enough.

Out of my penchant for artful clothing emerged a custom T-shirt with one of Peter's boat paintings silk-screened across the front that we both sported on the third day of the three-day event. It was a Saturday, and I set my office work aside to experience a day of art with Peter. The event was at a beautiful location, and the day was warm and sunny. The Monet hat was proving to be just the thing under the sun, and the new gear was working perfectly, including the wet panel carriers the artist had dipped into his considerable carpentry skills to build. He worked at top speed to put the finishing touches on the last two paintings so he could meet the mid-afternoon submission deadline.

"The pressure of the deadline forces me to speed up," he admitted to me quietly. "I need that sometimes. I'm not sure I could do these events week after week like some of these artists, though."

There was a time when I wouldn't have used "artist" and "pressure" in the same sentence, when my idea of an artist was more associated with free-spiritedness than with timely outcomes. It was a sign of how far I'd come that I simply nodded my understanding.

Peter's inroads with speed were not all that dazzled me that day. He exuded a new confidence. People milling around watching him work would, historically, have disconcerted him. Not today. Even the very persistent man who approached the easel again and again to interrupt the artist for a critique of his own amateur attempts did not break Peter's focus. I ran interference as much as possible.

"Thanks for distracting him," Peter said, turning to me as we drove over to deliver his wet paintings.

"Sure. I never realized how a well-meaning enthusiast could derail an artist," I confessed.

"I think people generally view painting as a hobby or pastime, not a profession," Peter answered thoughtfully. "They don't understand that, even at one of these events, professional artists have to produce to make a living. Our presence is picturesque, but we're working. We have to stay focused to finish the product."

This was another of those uncomfortable art-related truths I knew I'd never have learned from a book.

We found a place to wash up and change for the reception. I threw my brightly flowered scarf over my shoulder as we entered the packed show room buzzing with enthusiasts. Peter, like many of the other artists, sold most of his pieces, a great achievement for his first juried plein air event in Maine. His second great achievement still awaited discovery: Tasha the Terrible was safely behind bars when we pulled into the driveway that night.

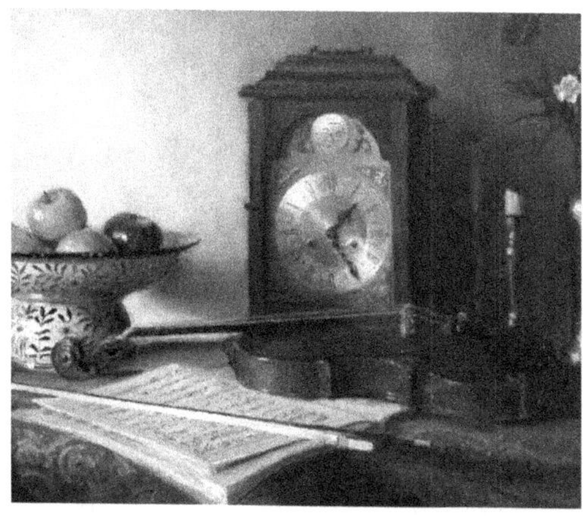

34

Art Strategies

"Half the money I spend on advertising is wasted;
the trouble is, I don't know which half."
—John Wanamaker

When the dust of our first summer in Maine settled, we took stock of our situation. It had been harder than we thought to leave our guests to their own devices, especially the grandkids.

"I'm really behind on my painting," Peter said. "We're going to have to manage our time better when we have guests. And," he added with emphasis, "you haven't had a single day to yourself yet this year."

He was right. It was already late August, near the end of the season. Between the demands of work and our many guests, the time had gotten away from us. We vowed not to let this happen again. Discipline, equally the artist's crucible and desideratum, seemed to me to be counter-intuitive to rest and rejuvenation. Yet, discipline was the only way we'd reserve time and energy for art and for ourselves. It was another of life's puzzling paradoxes.

I set aside my office work again one Saturday afternoon for our first annual Maine marketing meeting. Notably, this meeting did not take place at our traditional board room, the living room couch. Sipping a glass of chilled wine at a Belfast café table, I basked in the sun watching the boats and sparkling water and preparing to brainstorm ideas for Peter's future development and sales. Everything was on the table for discussion: web site, ads, galleries, networking, blog, juried shows, workshops, plein air shows, and art associations. On this occasion, I cracked open a new notebook labeled simply "Art", closed my eyes, and inhaled the intoxicating scent of the new paper like a junkie. Peter sniggered as I began to take notes.

"A fresh record for a fresh start," came my defensive reply. "Your reboot in Maine merits separate billing."

He conceded my point.

Our first task was to review the last twelve months. Since we'd arrived in Maine, despite the demands of garden, house and me, Peter had been accepted into two more Maine galleries, expanding his representation from Bar Harbor to Portland. He'd boldly taken a dozen paintings and approached one gallery whose owner had admired a plein air painting in progress last summer. Success! Likewise, he'd knocked on the doors of others whose collections seemed fitted to his style. He'd been juried into the American Impressionist Society show, exhibited in several Maine shows and painted a collection of seascapes and boat scenes from up and down the coast. His new work included iconic locations such as Mt. Desert Island, Schoodic Point, Castine, Cape Elizabeth and the famous Stonington yellow house. He'd painted a great variety of imagery—ocean waves, lobster boats, schooners, beaches at low tide—that screamed "Maine", on all canvas sizes. I'd never seen Peter more content, nor his work so good.

"Looks like we made the right decision," I observed, smiling over at him. "I guess we can take moving back to Omaha off the list of possibilities," I teased, feigning to strike it from the page.

When I said "we", I meant it literally. I had contributed as much, in my way, to Peter's artistic evolution as he had himself, and I felt invested in every inch of progress he made, just as I shared the pain of his setbacks.

The second task was to lay out a plan for the upcoming year. I jumped in first, not wanting the artist to spend another winter in the dark and knowing he'd never make the suggestion himself.

"We need to get more light into that studio. Let's replace that solid door with one with a window and get a properly fitted storm door with good screening so you can open up even in the cold weather."

Satisfied with this renovation plan, we moved on.

"What areas do you want to target for galleries?" I waited, pen poised.

"I think it's smart to stick to the region for now," Peter reflected. "That holds true for plein air events, too. I'll still try for some national shows. I'm going to submit *Whitewater* to be juried for the next American Impressionist Society exhibit."

"Any area of Maine you want to visit or concentrate on?"

"Yes, I want to get up north into the County this fall," he answered.

And so went the discussion, though it turned again and again to production rate.

"It was so obvious at the plein air event," he said with typical honesty. "I painted faster than ever but still struggled to meet the deadline. Other artists didn't." His point was well taken. To keep up at plein air events, he would have to accelerate.

"Stick with it," I encouraged him. "Quality first. You're not one of the art-is-what-I-can-get-away-with painters, so short-cutting is not the solution. The speed will come. You're already ten times faster than you were, and you're better off painting one excellent piece than several that are mediocre. What can you do other than keep striving and give it time?" I asked earnestly.

"Nothing," he said, "except maybe stop pressuring myself so hard." He made a face as I jotted that idea into the book. It's always risky giving this woman a pen.

The marketing meeting was not only about Peter, it turned out.

"I hate not being more available for you," I lamented, keenly feeling our contracted time together generally and particularly over art. "I am always buried in office work, and it takes me so long before I have mental energy to even look at a painting. When I do, this second set of eyes you depend on is so bleary, I'm not sure it's any help at all." Looking directly into his blue eyes, I confessed painfully, "It's not letting up, you know. I don't think I'm going to make five years. I may not even make two."

I turned to stare out at the water. *In Omaha,* I thought, *I was simply tired. Here, I'm entirely subsumed by work pressures to the point of hardly recognizing myself. I'm out of touch with all the things I love: home, gardening, writing, art…and Peter. I barely recognize myself.* So exhausted was I, so all-consuming was my job, that the mere idea of making a change, however desirable, overwhelmed my overspent mind. I looked again at Peter.

"We came to Maine to live. I'm not living; I'm surviving."

He answered gently.

"We never said five years. We said we'd see. And you've lost track of Section 2A, the flexibility provision. It's boilerplate in every plan, short or long, don't forget. When you're done, you're done, and we'll figure it out. I remember someone saying that to me not very long ago."

I smiled weakly.

"I think it's come to that," I said, "but I'll finish out the year. It would be irresponsible to do otherwise." I paused and threw up my hands. "I don't even know what I want. Just not this," I told him, trying hard to keep from breaking down in a public place. "I'm going to need help."

"Anything," he responded, reaching for my hand.

"Thanks." I looked into his sympathetic face. "In the meantime…I mean, until I can make a change…I'm worried I'm letting our partnership down."

"How can you even say that?" Peter asked, incredulous.

"Because I've worked on this art venture for years, just like you have, and the thought of neglecting it only weighs me down further." I paused to take a deep breath. "Do you remember the van Gogh-ish daily painting of a grocery list you called *Before She Calls?*" I asked Peter. "You blogged back then that, after thirty years, we were so in sync that you knew when I would call and had the pencil and list ready to jot things down." He laughed at the memory of it. "Well, after years of working so closely together in art, I have become tuned to you, too, and the little things that help you bring out your best. And it hurts when I can't give them."

Peter understood what I meant.

There were intimate things about him, like the quadrants of the canvas grid his astigmatic eye naturally favored, when distractions were interfering with his focus, and his body language when he got stuck. There were also innate skills that I brought to the table: an inner horizon that caught skewed perspective, a sense of design that picked up composition imbalance, and a critical eye that zoomed in on brush strokes and other detail. I had some idea of color and could spot washed out patches and weak lines. Most important of all, I'd assimilated Peter's training to the point of being able to critique a work according to his own sophisticated check points: central point of interest, geometry, narrative, contrast, values and so on. My complete preoccupation with office work meant he did not have these tools readily at his disposal.

"I would feel better if you kept a checklist for when I'm not around," I said a bit more brightly, "so you're not held up by me."

"OK," was all he said.

Frankly, I think Peter would have run with anything I wanted in that moment. With his help, I regurgitated all he had taught me into the Art notebook, then distilled it down into a simple quality assurance checklist he willingly pinned to his easel. I left for work on Monday in the hope that Peter would be better off with my little checklist and in the certain knowledge that he would never tell me otherwise.

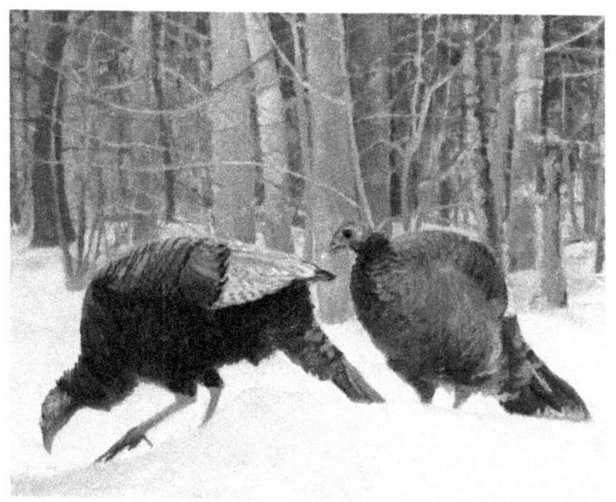

35

Artmobile

In the final months of that year, Peter's old pick up, the art wagon, was downgraded to snow plow, and the search began for a new vehicle. We ended up with a used Toyota Sienna van. As if to seal the destiny of this vehicle, Peter immediately slapped a "Plein Air Painters of Maine" sticker on the back bumper and promptly christened the van in several places with paint smudges.

"I can fit everything in here!" he said excitedly after the test drive. "We can fit the grandkids or even camp in the back!" He threw a hopeful look at me. "And it's got all-wheel drive. You can drive it to work on the really bad snow days."

His salesmanship was a hoot. I caught a glimpse of the owner who, eyes smiling at the ease of the sale, wisely let Peter do all the talking. Not a novice to collaborative car buying, Peter made sure I got behind the wheel and gave my approval before closing the deal.

The artmobile would clearly be the dominion of the artist who, in case I had any doubt about priorities, immediately yanked out the back seats and filled the space with art gear. It was not long before he could not remember life without this spacious, multi-purpose studio-on-wheels. He even painted from inside it when it rained. Occasionally, he was required to accede to the rights of joint ownership and hand his partner the wheel. I did my best to close my eyes to the chaos behind the seats and to return the van to its primary driver as promptly as possible. My sole stipulation was that the seats themselves be kept paint-free, though I knew from the start I'd have to allow for at least a ten per cent deviation.

Among its other applications, the artmobile quickly became indispensable as a delivery van. With larger canvases and exhibits in more places, its ample space was a godsend.

"This thing is so comfortable," I remarked on our first art trek together in the van.

"Good for long trips," Peter added. "I'm hoping to use it to join paint-outs with other artists. It'll be perfect." I listened intently to his continuing monologue, sensing that he was on the brink of an alteration in course of some kind. "There's a lot to be gained over social media and email," he maintained, "but there's nothing like working side by side with other artists. That's what I love about meetings of the Plein Air Painters of Maine and workshops and all the other places I've met artists."

I'd seen the benefit of these meetings first hand. Among his peers, Peter became animated, inspired and focused. He gained knowledge. He improved his skills. And notably, he returned in kind. If the artmobile was instrumental in making more of these meetups possible, it was worth every penny.

He held true to his promise of sharing the artmobile on snowy days. Travel during our second winter in Maine, another extreme season, though precarious, was less arduous rolling through the snow in what was tantamount to a tank compared to the little hatchback. Between the superiority of this hardy vehicle and the many changes we'd made to our place in the last year, the second winter took comparatively less effort, and I appreciated the reduction in stress.

One bitter and blowing night, Peter met me at the door looking strangely taller than usual. He dropped his mirthful eyes to his feet, which were stuffed deep inside a new pair of monstrous arctic "moon" boots.

"These were recommended for extreme temperatures by Stapleton Kearns, the New England painter I've admired who's teaching the winter workshop," he announced, comically rocking back and forth on the three-inch soles.

I shook my head. No matter how much you have, there's always more art gear.

The mental image I formed of Peter in the huge boots, his black, one-piece snowsuit and his old ski cap pulled over his face was, frankly, a bit scary. As if he read my mind, he did a little Frankenstein-stepping over to the couch to pull the boots off.

"They're ridiculous," I laughed, "but if they work…" I shrugged and let that thought dangle, rushing to voice my excitement of his upcoming introduction to more New England artists.

January arrived in a cold blast, though we would later discover that winter had not yet wielded its worst. One night, I arrived safely home, thanks to the artmobile, and, still standing in the doorway in my snow-covered coat, blurted, "I'm finished with this job. I just can't do it anymore."

Peter waited patiently through the rush of emotion that inevitably follows a declaration of this kind. The first wave of tears and breathless frustration. The second wave of guilt and self-justification. The third of fatigue and resignation.

"I usually know when I'm done with a thing, but my mind is so blurry." I stopped to calm my breathing. "This job got us to Maine," I choked, revealing the core of my inner conflict. "It's been a gift, and I've done my best to honor that gift. You've done everything you can to take the stress off me, including share the artmobile." I released a giggle. "I'm willing to keep working," I assured him, "at something less exhausting. I really think I've given all I can to this place. I just want to be sure I'm not walking away prematurely."

I looked up at him pleadingly, distrusting my own judgment. I needed to hear his.

"It's time," he said simply with mind-boggling calm and clarity.

"You're the most responsible person I know. You've done three years of duty in a year and a half's time without losing your gratitude. You've persevered so well that you've made even me believe you still had the will to go on. I've been poking around for jobs since our marketing meeting, but we'll start looking more aggressively now, this time for something better suited to the person you've become."

I dropped my head onto his shoulder. This was not the proverbial "we". When Peter said "we", he meant it. Partners in joint search for the right fit. Without telling me, he even searched for himself. I continued to roll the artmobile to and from the office on the snowy roads in the comforting awareness that the Job Whisperer was back at work.

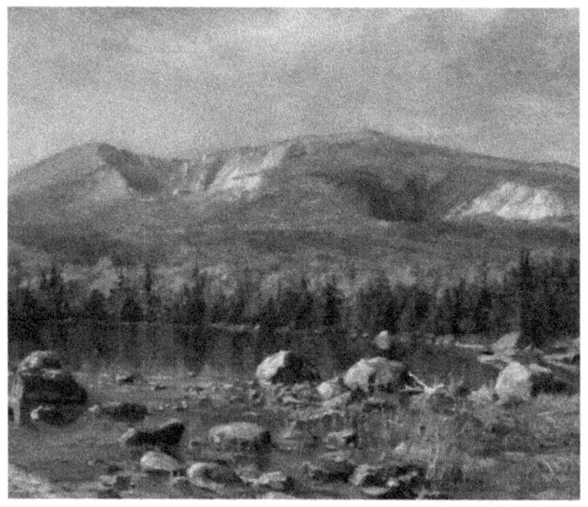

36

Balance

"I put my heart and soul into my work and have lost my mind in the process."
—Vincent van Gogh

In the months that followed, Maine was hit by winter storm after winter storm, further extending my work days. Just to make it to the office, I was forced to turn my limited energy away from the job search to focus on clearing Old Man Winter's snow piles. Finally, the relentless storms subsided, and the hard winter gave way to a welcome spring. The interviews began, though the process was slow. Everyone seemed to be behind and still recovering from the weather. *One day at a time*, I repeated to myself as I dragged my weary body from bed each morning.

In the meantime, Peter was grappling with a vexing question that put him in a state of upheaval as well, and not for the first time: *For whom am I painting?* Each time he picked up a blank canvas, the question rose before him like a specter. We had pondered it together at intervals ever since he had turned professional, and its complexity and evolving nature surprised us. In Omaha, galleries had advised him to choose popular subjects, pointing him toward their own ideas of marketable art: urban scenes and the big sky. Now, he was receiving guidance from Maine galleries.

"I don't take fog paintings," one gallery informed the bewildered artist, handing back a painting of a lighthouse in a soft mist with the lantern fittingly aglow.

"There's beauty in mood," Peter ruminated as he rehung the piece on our Great Gallery wall. "Isn't fog the reason we have lighthouses?"

On his next visit to the same gallery, there were three fog paintings on the wall by other artists.

Another gallery warned, "I can't sell boat paintings unless the boats are in the water."

Peter took them back. The same gallery sold several paintings of boats in dry dock by other artists that very year.

With confusing indications like these and multiple galleries to please, Peter had to carefully plan his choice of subject matter while continually checking his inner artist.

"Having my heart in the piece is going to produce the best outcome," he repeated over and over like an affirmation.

Appealing to his artist network, he found that others grappled with the *For whom am I painting?* puzzle as well, though knowing he had company did nothing to ease his own discord.

"I want to paint what I want to paint," he told me bluntly, then, after a thoughtful pause, added, "I also need to sell."

"Artists of old painted to pay the bills, didn't they?" I asked. "They had to please their patrons to live."

"They also painted for themselves. Well, the impressionists, anyway," his mulling went on. "Though they didn't necessarily make money in their lifetimes. Professional art, especially representational art, isn't only about self-expression, though to my mind, the inner artist has to play a critical role."

Maintaining equilibrium in art between personal gratification and financial means, it seemed to me, was like walking on Mount Katahdin's Knife Edge Trail. It took the combined forces of steadiness, self-discipline and inspiration. The issue became a hot topic among the artist and his Council of Four.

"Maybe you need to re-phrase the question," suggested our daughter, ever tuned to the inner man. "Try asking 'Why am I painting?'"

Discussions ensued over the forces driving artists to paint including, in Peter's case, to remind viewers that this difficult world is also beautiful.

"Interpreting beauty," Peter seized the word. "This is where I began."

"Has this intent really changed over all these years of painting?" I wanted to understand.

"No," he replied emphatically. "Quite the opposite."

"Then, this is the thing to hold onto. When you get muddled, just click to return to the default settings," I added, attempting some humor to offset these sober reflections.

For whom am I painting? could not be put to rest from the standpoint of subject matter alone. *For whom?* concerns not only the product itself but its intended audience. "Audience" is a broad term in today's art world, including collectors, gallery visitors, web site and social media viewers and event attendees, among others. As carefully as an artist must choose what to put on canvas, he must also consider the response to it from a myriad of potential sales perspectives.

"I got an invitation from another fund-raiser," Peter told me over dinner. Requests for donations of artwork were increasing in frequency. That the causes were worthy was a given, but the artist's contribution was not so straightforward.

"Should we consider these compliments, signs that you're making a name for yourself?" I suggested brightly.

"Not necessarily," came his truthful answer. "They're probably inviting every artist they can find to maximize their auction material."

"Auctions are different from other venues for the artist, aren't they?" I asked. "A co-worker once bragged to me that he'd purchased the painting of a well-known Maine artist at a very low price. That kind of thing can't be good for artists."

"No," concurred Peter, "If the auction doesn't set a minimum bid, the artist is underselling himself as well as the galleries who represent him. Much as I value the programs, I can't just give work away. I have to honor my gallery representation. And I have to make a living."

How quickly the loftiness of the inner artist and the charitable donation can dissolve into a tug of war with day-to-day needs.

After so many years in the field, I could run the figures in my head: the cost of the canvas, paint, framing, delivery, travel, the commission and, so often overlooked, the artist's production time. Donating just one painting is the equivalent of working a few days at a job without pay, I calculated. It could even equate to a few weeks' pay depending upon the size and complexity of the painting. How many people would give up that much potential income as frequently as artists are invited to do so?

I turned my attention back to Peter, who'd moved on to plein air events, which posed the same problem as the auctions.

"The causes they support are great," Peter asserted, "but they take a lot of production time with no guarantee of sales. And there is the additional cost of travel and even housing, for some."

"I don't think most people appreciate what goes into a painting, particularly a representational work," I guessed, "and I'm absolutely sure most don't realize you can't even deduct your donation! Remember when we thought the art profession was just a matter of paint well and sell?"

We both laughed.

As his experience with them grew, Peter began to evaluate art events more closely. Always moved by the world around him, it pained him to approach good causes in a dispassionate, calculated manner. This was, after all, the artist who'd painted memorials for the September 11 disaster (*Peace*), for the Miyako City tsunami victims (*For Miyako*) and for veterans (*The Veteran*). He'd also worked to memorialize the College World Series' Rosenblatt Stadium (*Rosenblatt*) and other historical sites before they were torn down or developed. And he'd outright donated numerous paintings. Now, he researched extensively before making a commitment—artist participation and style, buyer attendance, volume of sales and sale prices.

"Maybe the best measure is the extent of the exposure you get at the plein air event as an artist," I suggested.

"It's one," he agreed. "Another has to be if the event is in a location at which I want to paint. I have to know I will be able to find inspiration there and also be able to sell that subject in my galleries if it isn't sold at the event. And," he looked up at me earnestly, "I have to be OK with travel. Several artists I know are away from home eight to ten months out of the year with all these events. That's not the lifestyle I want."

"Yeah, that's not much better than joining the art fair circuit we rejected years ago in Des Moines, unless you want to change your mind about getting a Winnebago," I teased.

He laughed.

"I may be happier if I just decide which causes I support the most and limit my contribution to those."

Faced with these difficult questions, I felt acutely the inadequacy of being an *UN*-painting art partner. No doubt, I could track the conundrum intellectually, measure it financially and sympathize warmly with the artist's plight, but not equally to a fellow artist. Only a peer could truly understand the blood, sweat and tears, the personal risks, and the emotional complexity of this narrow path between the need for sales and the inner artist. While my gifts were unique and those only an intimate partner could give, this was clearly a line I could not cross.

As the artmobile rolled on toward a new gallery in Connecticut, I encouraged Peter to seek out peers more often.

"You need to pack up and take this thing wherever they're congregating," I urged him.

The topic was not coincidental. I had offered to share the drive, and we'd stopped for what was my first exposure to life at an historical art colony, the home of Florence Griswold that had housed the early 20th century Old Lyme artists. I'd had the perfect tour guide in Peter, who was familiar with all the old art colonies. He recited their history and influence as we stepped through the Griswold house, recalling to me New Hope, Pennsylvania, Cape Ann, Massachusetts and Monhegan Island off the coast of Maine as other examples.

"I have a professional network," I remarked after taking in Old

Lyme. "The art colony seems like a much more intimate experience. Real bonds are forged. It's more community than network, it seems."

Perhaps I was being overly idealistic, but to me, Old Lyme was exactly the model Peter needed to maintain an even keel.

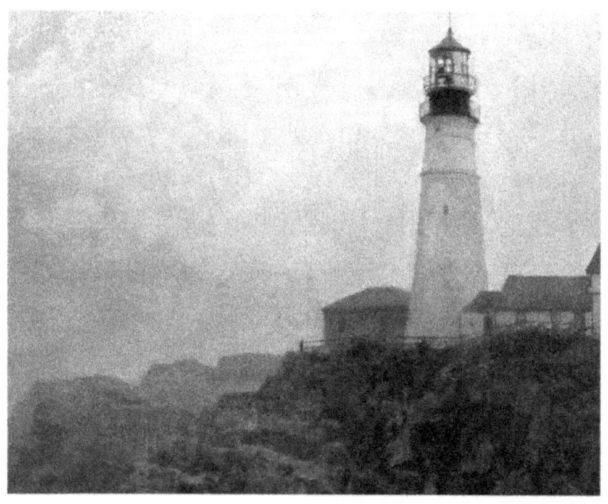

37

Mood

"If you could say it in words, there would be no reason to paint."
—Edward Hopper

By late spring, I worked the last day at the life-numbing job.

"Thank God you're out of there." Peter surrounded me with his arms as I got out of the car. "Thank God," he repeated emphatically, audibly sighing a depth of relief I shared.

I basked in his comfort, still carrying the weight of the whole experience, yet aware that this was not just an end; it was also a beginning.

After a long embrace, he leaned back and said, "Change your clothes!" then rushed me off to the bayside for a picnic supper. "I know it's tempting but I don't think you should accept the job offer you just received," he advised me firmly over gourmet cheese and fresh fruit. "You should take the whole summer off. You are worn so thin. You need to recover before you take something else on."

Normally, I'd have run off a list of practical objections. It was a testament to the extremity of my emotional and mental fatigue that I simply acquiesced. Peter was absolutely right. I needed to recharge. I would be no good to a new employer in my present condition.

"My only caveat," I said, "is that I want to get right into the community. I've not met a soul in our area except our nearest neighbors and a few of your art friends. I want to connect."

The next day, I slept in luxuriously, then dressed to go volunteer my services and to begin, for the first time since we'd moved in, to truly experience Maine first hand. Standing on the Belfast wharf, I basked in the blues and greens of the water, inhaled the salty air and felt the breezes against my face. *This is why you came to Maine*, I reminded myself.

At home, I dove into gardening, but so great was my exhaustion that my mind and hands seemed disconnected, like I was watching someone else do the work. I stopped short from breathlessness during yard work and on hikes and fell asleep on the couch mid-afternoons. It was absolutely terrifying to apprehend the dearth of my energy. Fear compelled me to take this recovery period very seriously.

Nothing was more gratifying or exhilarating that summer than the moment when I pulled my writing out of hibernation. Grinning widely at Peter, I ceremoniously unsealed the moving box I had not opened since it had been taped shut back in Omaha and spilled the whole pile of journals onto the living room floor. Jane Austen will excuse me, I hope, in imagining my own longing and happiness to be akin to hers when she pulled her dear writing box out of the attic after a long hiatus.

"It's the closest I'll ever come to approaching her writing," I admitted.

It felt like heaven nevertheless.

I could also rejoice that I was now free to be more active in art again and quick to be on hand when Peter uttered a disgruntled "Ugh!" from the computer chair. He bent his forehead to the table in a mock attempt to beat out his frustration. Across the screen was a single sentence meant to begin his artist biography for an upcoming event.

"Why can't I just paint and let the work speak for itself?" he asked out loud. "I never know what to say in these things," he complained, "and I can't just keep recycling the old text."

Words never had been Peter's bailiwick, especially if they were about himself. Ask him to paint a self-portrait, and he'd reveal all he had to say with aplomb. Ask him to construct a few autobiographical sentences, and he was quickly defeated.

I slid next to him at the computer.

"People want to know about the creator of the piece they buy and where he is in his art journey. You look up artists' backgrounds all the time. This means bios," I said softly. "Step away from the keyboard for a minute so you can get clear, and let's just talk in concepts."

We sat together, Peter generating thoughts as I keyed them.

"Now," I said when he ran out of steam, "give me a few minutes to tie these ideas together."

A short time later, I walked back to the studio and presented him with a few paragraphs ordering his ideas. He made a few final edits, then sighed his relief that the thing was done. I smiled my contentment. We were side by side in art again.

A stream of guests was lined up for the summer whom I would be able to fully enjoy. I made plans for a chocolate, moose-shaped birthday cake for our grandkids, read voraciously, sipped wine in the backyard and gardened to my heart's content. There were picnics by the water to attend, berries to pick, and greens to harvest. Determined to show me the Maine I had been missing during my "tour of duty" as he called it, Peter took me on frequent drives to galleries and scenic destinations where he'd painted, with the occasional spontaneous detour.

"Look!" he exclaimed as we entered Port Clyde. "It says 'art show'!"

We veered onto the back road indicated by the sign, craning our necks to find the exhibit. It turned out to be a small, informal affair in the front yard of a large house shared by artists who had gathered for a few weeks to paint together. A summer art colony. What a find. Peter was warmly welcomed and quite drawn in.

"They're realists!" he burst with excitement as we slid back into the artmobile. "And they invited me back!"

It wasn't Old Lyme, but it was as close as he'd come so far.

Among our guests that summer were our son and daughter-in-law who joined Peter and me at a plein air event in southern Maine. The final day of the event was scorching. Peter labored under both Monet hat and sun umbrella on a rather difficult rocky beach scene, draining bottles of water against the heat. His entourage lounged lackadaisically around him except for the moment when, in a fit of heat exhaustion, I spontaneously plunged into the waves, clothes and all. After a brief waterside picnic, the artist resumed work until the submission deadline. As we all helped him pack up, he looked over his work and summed up his discouragement.

"I could have used more time," he said.

It was the largest canvas Peter had ever attempted at a plein air event, an achievement unto itself. He had not finished to his usual degree of detail. He had nevertheless managed a fine painting and something else rather arresting: *mood.* He had always maintained that his style of realism was intentionally not photographic. He wanted feeling and mood like Whistler's paintings and Homer's seascapes, and the mood of this painting was his strongest yet. It was as if all the imagery simultaneously held its form yet melted together into a single vibration. This was another turn of the development spiral, and even Peter could not help but celebrate it, after he cooled his head.

The season ended on a high note in every sense of the word, as Peter completed his first painting of Mount Katahdin. Mood had been the theme this summer. Mine was elated. Our guests were euphoric. And Peter had found it through his brush. When he and I reconvened at the seaside café for our second annual marketing meeting, trusty Art notebook opened to a clean page, it was hard not to grin at how far we'd both come in recent months toward the lifestyle we'd been craving. Peter had disciplined himself into several new galleries as well as regional and national exhibitions and had broadly expanded his peer network. I had found a job, again in business management, so tailor-made to my needs that I couldn't have designed it better myself. Fifteen-minute drive. Normal hours. Small, friendly business. Just enough challenge.

Just as our last guests of the season departed, I pulled the car out of the garage for my first day with my new employer.

"A whole summer in Maine to rest, and now another beginning," I said to Peter through the driver's door window, flushing pink with gratitude through my summer tan. "For me, it's like being transported back to the day we first slid out of that smelly moving truck to start our new life."

Rubbing my hands together in newfound energy, I couldn't wait to see what the next year would bring.

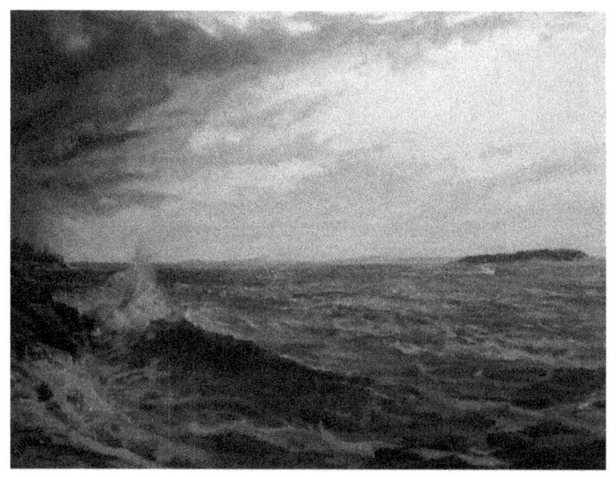

38

Art Community

"The pessimist complains about the wind;
the optimist expects it to change;
the realist adjusts the sails"
—William Arthur Ward

Fall quickly dissipated into our third winter in Maine, and my shorter trek to work as well as the emptier roads in the off season were a godsend in the bad weather. By now, Peter was really getting the hang of the tourist season which, in Maine, ignited on Memorial Day and was already flickering out by mid-September. A number of galleries did not stay open in the off season. Accepting this reality, he persevered in his quest to expand representation and exposure to other markets while the snow whipped all around the house.

"I have a list of galleries I want to try," he said, turning to me. "Of course, I have to feed each gallery." He paused, mentally adding up the number of paintings he would have to produce and breathed out a momentary panic. "The plein air events are great venues, too," he added, "but long and exhausting in themselves without calculating in the travel time."

"We're back to the time management theme, it seems." I looked up from writing and cocked my head to one side. "Are you aware of the amount of time you spend on Facebook?"

"Yeah," he replied in frustration. "Acutely aware. I'm using it instead of the blog now. It's a great tool but so full of distractions that I have to sift through a lot of irrelevant material to get to the art posts, which is the only reason I'm there."

I frowned sympathetically. Internet self-promotion is a must in the contemporary market. Even artists who retained or rebuilt their gallery representation after the economic downturn realize its value. All the internet tools at artists' disposal—web sites, art forums, advertising, exhibitions and social media—are required to remain in the game, plus the new fad of the moment. In addition to Facebook, Peter built a painting library on Pinterest. He also moved his solo web site to the popular *FineArtStudioOnline* collective.

"It's where buyers seem to be now," he explained, "and certainly other artists and enthusiasts."

Keeping up with web trends, browsing for opportunities and maintaining existing platforms are necessities of the time that take precious hours away from the studio.

"With all the time I spend posting, responding, searching and building, it's a wonder I have time to paint," he complained. "I need to keep my work out there and stay connected to other artists."

Watching him scroll for meaningful material, I mentally calculated that whatever Peter gained in an hour on Facebook could be gained in the space of a few minutes in the company of his peers.

"And I'd rather spend this time painting with other artists," he admitted, intuiting my train of thought.

If Peter was any indication, professional artists not only yearn for peer meetings, they need to congregate. The need arises from something more than mere enjoyment of the creative process and the social opportunities it affords. Professionals, like amateurs and hobbyists, appreciate these things but also rely on one another for an indispensable and cathartic exchange related to their trade. Professional peers are trusted sources of constructive feedback, reliable suppliers and firsthand views of the latest pricing and marketing trends. They help one another over obstacles and low points. All the years spent taking advantage of technology had not diminished Peter's preference for meet-ups. In fact, the need to mingle had actually amplified in proportion to his achievements.

Winter gave way to spring, and Peter was invited to paint a piece inspired by a Hudson River school artist for the Acadia National Park Centennial. He chose Thomas Cole's *View Across Frenchman's Bay After a Squall*. After some research, he went to Mount Desert Island to explore where Cole might have stood to sketch this scene.

"Wanna come?" he invited.

I jumped into the artmobile. Like a couple of detectives, we collected clues all along the water's edge. Cole's tendency to shift scenery in his compositions made pinpointing the precise spot difficult.

"This looks really, really close," said Peter, looking through a rectangle formed with his thumbs and index fingers, "assuming Cole relocated those distant islands to make them fit."

The similarity was unmistakable. Having identified the view, Peter set out to capture light and mood reminiscent of Cole. There's something intimidating about painting in the shadow of an old master, but he pulled it off nicely. The exercise drew him into Cole's world for a while, which fanned his already glowing flame for the intimate peer connections achieved at the old art schools and colonies.

On behalf of the artist, I quietly took up the mouse myself to browse for art meet-ups in the region. "Check this out," I called when he returned to the great room to refill his tea cup. I'd stumbled upon an old computer game called *Artist Colony* (Nikitova Games 2009).

"Looks a little hokey. The goal is to build an art community, apparently by applying some of those time management skills you and I have been talking about," I laughed.

As a skill-building tool, I can't say if the game was effective. It's far more captivating feature in my estimation was the dangling carrot of peer relationships it pretended to offer. The game itself was merely a collection of zeroes and ones. Its machinations, though, played to an emotional reality: artists' desire for esprit de corps. People will play at anything, it seems, including community, but I had witnessed the real thing between artists.

Up-close and personal comradery may be the ultimate endgame, but the great irony is that peer relationships can no longer be contemplated without a tip of the brush to the digital connections on which they now depend.

"I've yet to meet an artist who doesn't depend on a smart phone to stay plugged into the peer network," Peter said.

"Yeah, digital community," I reflected, "sounds like an oxymoron, you know, considering the impersonality of the internet as opposed to the intimacies of meet-ups. Digital networking is an undeniable fact of art life now. Part of the internet's charm, I think, is that it's casual, expedient and pretty democratic."

"Yeah," he agreed, "and in-person networking, like colonies, residencies, workshops, plein air events and exhibits, are often limited by peer invitation, juried acceptance or even funds."

"What's the best answer, then, to getting artists to meet up just to exchange ideas?" I asked him.

"Gatherings," he replied without hesitation. "Gathering" had become Peter's label for in-person get-togethers of varying length and size where artists converged to paint, eat, talk art and then paint, eat and talk art some more.

"Go," I urged him at every opportunity. "There are football widows and hunting widows in the season, so I guess from time to time, I'm willing to be an art widow." He opened his mouth to respond, but I anticipated him. "No, I don't enjoy being without you," I quickly admitted, "but you need to be with peers without always having me in tow." I never had to tell him twice.

As spring gave way to the summer art season, gatherings rose to predominance in both conversation and opportunity as if responding to Peter's call. He shared WikWak cottage, a historic converted fishing house on Monhegan Island, with fellow artists for a week and also joined peers in the Vermont hills and at Port Clyde, Boothbay and the Schoodic Peninsula. He expanded his participation to new locations with a history of art appreciation such as Cape Ann, Massachusetts and Bucks County, Pennsylvania. I took all this activity down in my journal like a documentarian during the widowhood intervals and, once in a while, jumped into the artmobile (or ferry) to join him. Partnerships do have their perks.

Setting down my pen to watch the sun set from WikWak's porch overlooking the sea, I observed to Peter, "You know, I've been looking through my journals and I have a lot of material about your journey as an artist and all we have learned together. It would make an interesting story, maybe even an educational one."

"Really?" was all he said.

I took that as a "yes".

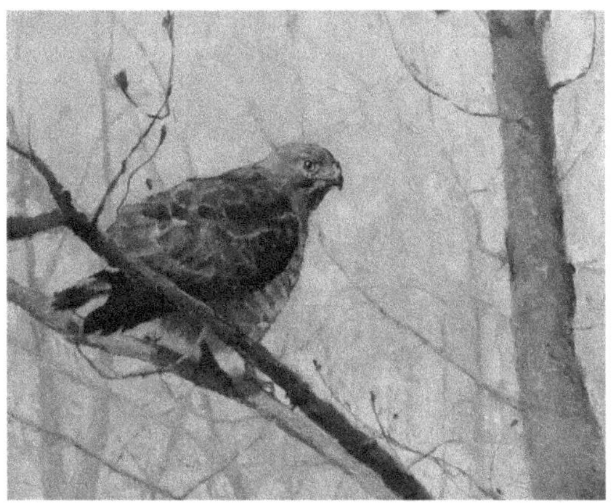

39

Art of Zen

*"As my artist's statement explains, my work is utterly incomprehensible
and is therefore full of deep significance"*
—Calvin, Bill Watterson, *Calvin and Hobbes*

I got up to stretch from crafting stories and tip-toed into the quiet studio. I approached Peter softly, not wanting to startle him as he sat motionless in front of his easel, light streaming across his lap from a newly installed studio window.

"What are you doing?"

I waited the few seconds it took for him to answer.

"Meditating," he said simply, then added, "It's sort of a Zen thing."

I stifled my curiosity and left him to it but welcomed his explanation later over dinner.

"I've been thinking about the quality of my work," he began, "and how my artistic voice translates beauty. There are external measures for a painting. Does it even look like the subject? Does it compel you to look? Is it marketable? Did it get good feedback? Is it comparable to my peers' work? Internally, my measurement is, Does the painting evoke what I want to convey to others? Beauty is not the same as technical refinement; it's bigger than the thing you're looking at. There's a lot of art noise out there. It's like listening to mediocre music and then you hear Beethoven's 9th. I'm striving for the 9th. I want to play above the current. I need to reach more deeply when I work."

Wow.

We'd just concluded our third annual Maine marketing meeting. It hadn't even approached this scale of thinking. We'd talked about the strenuous season he'd had traipsing from one plein air event to another. We'd celebrated the upcoming Oil Painters of America exhibit of *What's for Dinner,* a painting of a hawk, Peter's first serious foray back into wildlife since his art school days. A debate over a bird and flower series had ensued. We'd made frequent, light-hearted detours from art to gush over the imminent birth of our second granddaughter. Nothing about that meeting had prepared me for the deep reflections that had just eloquently rolled off Peter's tongue over broccoli and broiled haddock.

From his most recent bout with the For-whom-am-I-painting? question, I should have recognized the signs of this oncoming introspection. Stewing usually preceded meaningful change. Now that I was tipped off, it was easy to look back at a conversation earlier in the week with greater comprehension.

"There's way more representational art in art publications than there was in the sixties," he'd claimed. "Even art classes back then didn't offer much other than abstract and free expression."

I'd laughed and reached for one of my earlier journals. Finding a dog-eared page, I'd said, "You just reminded me of your mantra when you first returned to art. 'Realism is the new avant garde', you told me."

"I remember that. It's definitely seeing a resurgence," he continued, "though I'm not sure I see it overtaking abstract and design work."

Peter's contemplation flowed in a continuous undercurrent, then rose to the surface unpredictably, often resuming the same topic on a different day as if there had been no interval of time in between.

"The plein air craze may have contributed to a renewed interest in realism," he theorized aloud. "Of course, the market is very saturated with plein air now, so who knows where that will go?"

His gaze shifted to the window signaling the mental percolation beneath his greying hair.

"I've always wondered," I joined in, "if, at some point, people would tire of trendy art, of having to figure out and explain that strange and enigmatic thing on their wall, though there is a certain social value in conversational pieces. Now, we're seeing abstract painters at plein air events. I just can't wrap my head around this combination. The whole point of plein air painting is to capture what you see—light, in particular—isn't it? The very definition of abstract art is that it does not attempt to represent external reality."

Peter was as confounded as I at this development.

"Unlike realists and impressionists, abstract artists seem less focused on being understood," he said, laughing. "They don't mind being enigmatic. So, I think you're safe there."

Several days later, when browsing for new representational artists, Peter remarked, "There's so much art out there, though clearly not all of the same quality."

"Must be tough for a buyer," I reflected. "With fewer brick-and-mortar galleries on hand to screen the art and facilitate the buying process and more art than ever to sift through, the discerning buyer has a lot more work to do." I turned to him and asked, "Who and where is the art buyer these days?" With wealth ever more concentrated, and middle class disposable income dwindling, the contemporary art-buying public was not easy to identify.

"I don't know," he answered frankly. "There are still avid, traditional collectors out there and even some patronage, although that population appears to be shrinking."

"I read that the up-and-coming art buyers are the Millenials," I said. "Do you think this is true?"

"I don't know," he repeated, his face screwed up in perplexity. "They're comfortable buying art online, that's for sure, though it's not clear that a strong internet presence translates into sales. Will Millenials become collectors or patrons in the style of their forebears? Who knows? Do they like realism? It's impossible to say right now with any degree of certainty. Some of them may have inherited an art collection, so why buy? Or, maybe they're not making the financial gains of the previous generations, so their incomes may not support art enthusiasm."

The discussion left us with more questions than answers.

Glamorous as I had once thought the art profession to be, I now classified it as more blue collar than elite. Artists have to grind away like any artisan to maintain their place in the great churning wheel of supply and demand.

"So, artists are facing more competition, an overabundant supply and an uncertain buying public," I summarized. "These are conditions that would tend to pit them against one another," I continued, turning to catch Peter's reaction.

"The artists I've met are competitive with themselves, with the quality of their work today over yesterday," he answered thoughtfully, "but to other artists, they are nothing but helpful. They just want to make a living." This was a remarkable assertion, and even more so in a depressed and competitive market flooded with work.

Despite the uncertainties, Peter was resolute in his determination to draw from the deeper motivation for his painting. I waited for some dramatic action to follow his musings and meditations and was not disappointed.

"What are those tags?" I asked, stepping into the disordered studio.

"Those are the three paintings that have priority," he told me. "I'm taking the others off the wall. Want to help? Being surrounded by unfinished work is distracting me."

I assisted, never one to argue against focus and as fascinated as ever with the ongoing progression of the inner artist. Once we'd rearranged his work, he turned to me.

"I've collected photos of the paintings I think are my best work in a folder. Would you mind looking at them to see if you agree with me? I'm going to use these as a checkpoint for every finished painting from now on."

I plopped into the desk chair. She-Who-Must-Not-Be-Named had long ago added the daring dimension of Art Critic to her repertoire and had been regularly enlisted as such ever since. This review would be a new turn of the spiral. Humming the 9th Symphony for inspiration, I combed through the folder and made a few suggestions. Peter unhesitatingly adopted them in an almost ruthless judgment of his own work. How else could he reach for the essential Beethoven?

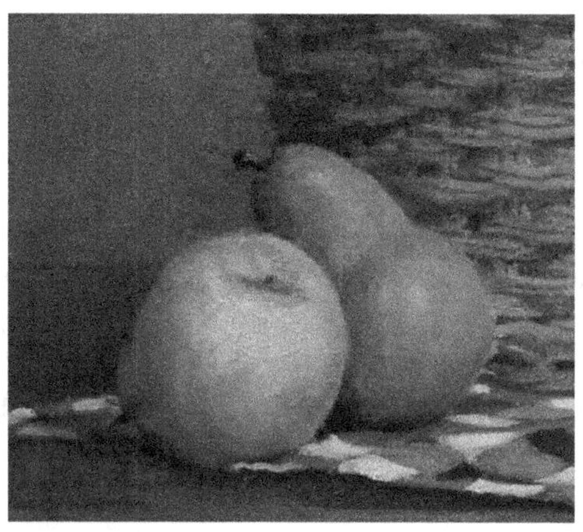

40

Finishing Touches

"The good life is a process, not a state of being. It is a direction not a destination."
—Carl Rogers

Change, especially when it ran as deep as his Zen undertaking, left Peter a bit rocky until his inner GPS caught up to his new art direction. I'd become accustomed to watching him navigate through uncertainty and self-doubt from the sidelines during these periods and talking him through the process. Change can be hard on the system but it also produces a stimulating buzz, a hyper-alertness and an adrenaline rush to spur you forward. At arm's length from the turmoil, I enjoyed the fresh energy generated by every inch of growth he achieved.

That summer, I'd joined Peter in a trip to Boothbay while he attended a plein air workshop taught by Don Demers, a realist renowned for his paintings of seascapes and historically accurate ships. I'd hung back, catching snippets of the class from a distance as an UN-painting artist, writing at intervals, and occasionally engaging in talk with the other students.

"I hear you're writing about Peter's journey as an artist," a dear and respected artist-friend remarked.

"Yeah, I have bits and pieces. It's not anything like a book yet." I paused and added tentatively. "But I'd like it to be."

"You need to get that book done," she returned matter-of-factly.

Her words, though spoken gently, struck me with force. I had all the pieces. What was I waiting for? Courage for one thing. Give me business writing, and I could whip out a finished product in minutes. Creative writing, especially about something so personal, was another thing altogether.

"I know you're the one in transformation," I told Peter a few weeks later as we sat warming on the enormous rock bed at Schoodic Point, "but I'm suddenly feeling full of anxiety, nervous and even fearful about the future. If I have to pick a word, I'd say I feel vulnerable. I can't seem to identify where all this emotion is coming from." I sat there looking at him from inside a cloud of my own. "Are you feeling this?" I asked him pointedly.

He stretched his legs out leisurely on the sun-bathed rock in front of a sea as restless as my insides and offered his reply without a second's hesitation.

"No, I'm not. And I know what your feeling is from. I've been watching you."

This startled me. Our positions were usually the other way around.

"You're not afraid of the future," he continued. "This is all about your writing. Vulnerability is what an artist feels every minute he paints because he's putting himself out there. One stroke looks like genius; the next is a failure." He looked at me curiously as he drew in his breath to deliver the punch line. "You are developing an artist's soul," he concluded confidently.

I stared at him, letting those words settle into my brain. If I was honest with myself, I had to admit they had a slight ring of truth. With writing, I had begun to "put myself out there", as Peter described it. I felt shaky, self-conscious and completely incompetent. As to the rest of his claim, I could not really say. An artist's soul? This seemed a bit lofty for me. I had always been the more left-brained of the two of us, the one who could tolerate the daily grind and wield a protective armor to survive in the world, one of the arguments I'd made for working outside the home for so long while Peter painted. This armor, I knew, had been giving way in recent years. I wasn't weaker; I had simply grown tired of wearing it. But an artist's soul?

"Are you an artist because you work as one or do you work as an artist because you are one?" the Council of Four had demanded of Peter years ago. Was I now facing the same question? I caught Peter's eyes and smirked.

"Does this mean I can leave the tea kettle on the stove to boil dry and put my pen in my coffee cup?"

He answered me with a spray of grapes. We laughed, and I felt an exhilaration similar to the one I'd felt on a beach in Nova Scotia years ago.

A few days later, Peter emerged from the studio.

"Mind if I interrupt you? I need a final review for the show."

He stepped back from the twenty canvases lined up around the periphery of the great room for a pre-show inspection. After a long hiatus, he was painting flowers again. Reviewing this work would be a joy. My job was to critique each individual piece and then the overall collection, as well as to supply a few titles. With my heightened sensitivity to the creative process, I approached this task not only with all my accumulated art knowledge but with increased empathy.

"I think this one needs a silver frame," I suggested, "and you might want to sharpen the edges of the petals right there."

The commentary went on as I stepped up to and back from each painting to offer precise feedback and then to remark on the show as a whole. Peter took it all in stride, counting on my observations to be sure he'd missed nothing. He would choose if and how to alter his work but he generally regarded my comments as valuable, at a minimum, for their freshness, having himself looked at the work too long. For us, this exercise had become routine, a natural process arising from our close partnership.

"I wouldn't want it any other way," he reassured me every time.

In mutual harmony, we boxed up the pieces, once again leaving behind empty and nail-pocked walls in the Great Gallery.

Our collaboration is certainly not unique to the art world. Many artists are assisted by significant others who contribute, as I do, their own particular strengths and skills to the enterprise. Certain aspects, like the act of painting itself, will always be beyond sharing (although we did once encounter two artists who painted the same canvas together), but the extraneous work in support of the painting itself can be a shared labor. Peter and I have enjoyed learning how other artists and their partners managed the load of research, web presence, purchasing, logistics, travel, finances, quality assurance, morale and so on. We reserve a special hats-off to those who are both content and successful managing solo, quite a feat knowing the amount of labor involved.

The intimacy of our art partnership is a testament to Peter, who patiently guided me through his world, freely shared his knowledge and open-heartedly welcomed my participation. The continual interchange between us by this time has become so ingrained, it is largely second nature. Only when we perceive a reaction to it does it again rise to the level of consciousness. From time to time, I have caught surprise on the face of an art acquaintance when the degree of my involvement in Peter's work becomes evident.

"I couldn't help seeing his expression when I joined the conversation about Peter's painting, though not a word was said," I told our daughter over Skype. "Not everyone is easy with our arrangement."

"They just don't know you yet," she defended us loyally, "and how well you've each supported the other in all things. They're seeing it narrowly in that moment only, as though you are the intruder. It's always been a two-way street. It's gotten so even I can't tell where one of you begins and the other ends, and not just in art." She paused thoughtfully. In anything, really."

Now that I thought about it, neither could I. Decisions about his paintings are ultimately the artist's. I've never lost track of this, but as we often complete one another's thoughts these days, it usually ends up the same.

The thread of close collaboration runs through every aspect

of our life, not just through art. A co-worker once told me that Peter's handling of the home front while I worked outside the home was a "role reversal". Peter's look was as quizzical as mine when I relayed the comment. Perhaps the man meant that the apportionment of work between us was rather untraditional.

"Do you give much thought to gender roles?" I asked Peter. "Are you uncomfortable with our division of labor?"

He answered flatly, "I've never felt the need to be constrained by someone else's idea of what I should be doing. I like the agility we have between us and the fact that each of us just does what's needed at the time regardless of that kind of artificial constraint. Labels," he observed, adding a grin, "like She-Who-Must-Not-Be-Named, of course, are just for fun."

"Yeah, that's how I see it, too," I said as I handed him my first manuscript to critique.

Just as I had ventured into art with Peter, he was about to enter the writer's world with me. Watching as he set aside his teacup, flipped to page one and uncapped his pen, I prepared to receive the same dose of honesty I had so often given to him. What goes around will inevitably come around in a dynamic relationship. I'd already come to rely on his help with my writing. If anything has strengthened our partnership, it has been this give and take, the unfixity of our parts in it. So many five-year plans have come and gone that I've lost count. Though we may subsist without a plan, we are never without the flexibility provision. Constant flexibility may be an oxymoron, but it is one of life's most potent forces if you figure out how to apply it effectively between you.

Even with all of the back and forth in our relationship, I am still surprised by the progression of my own journey. I began with the intention to write about playing second fiddle to an artist and ended up with a story as much about my own evolution as Peter's. He has undergone an amazing transformation, yet I sometimes feel I may have altered even more than he since that fateful day on the Nova Scotia sand. After all, I had been the art neophyte who'd embarked on this venture with a considerable deficit of knowledge and far more ground to cover. And it is only through supporting Peter's heart's desire that

I found my own.

Not enough credit in life is given to naiveté. Without it, we might never take a risk, and Peter and I might never have thrown ourselves into this crazy, wonderful scheme in joint pursuit of his art career. The journey is far from finished; we both continue in forward motion, ever undulating with the ups and downs of the creative world and the course adjustments it requires.

Despite the dynamics, some things are as constant as the day is long. Peter still dresses like a roving yard sale and leaves paint smudges all over the house. He still buys too many brushes and gets overwhelmed by new endeavors. For my part, I still spot crooked horizons from ten feet away, pull painting titles out of a hat and bite my tongue at art shows. And I am still scribbling every chance I get. Above all that has endured in this endeavor, we are still exactly where we want to be, side by side.

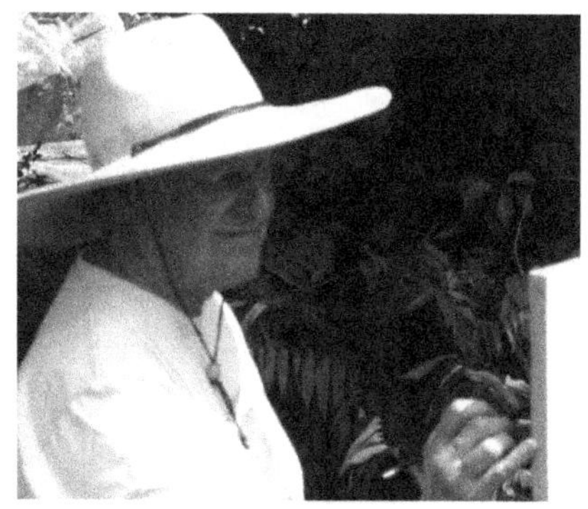

peteryesisart.com

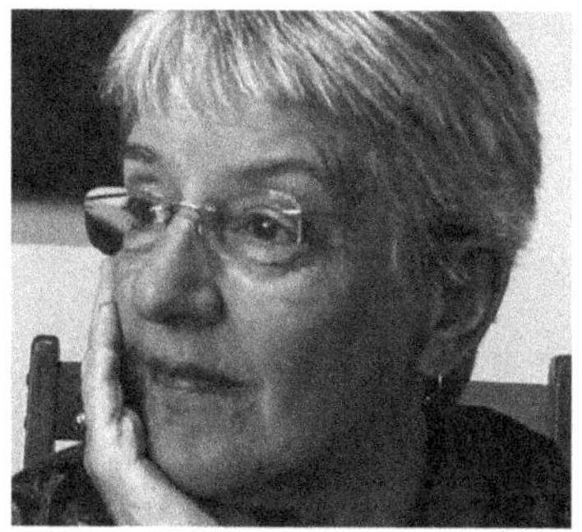

kimyesis.com

KIM YESIS writes from her home, where she lives with her husband and creative partner, artist Peter Yesis.

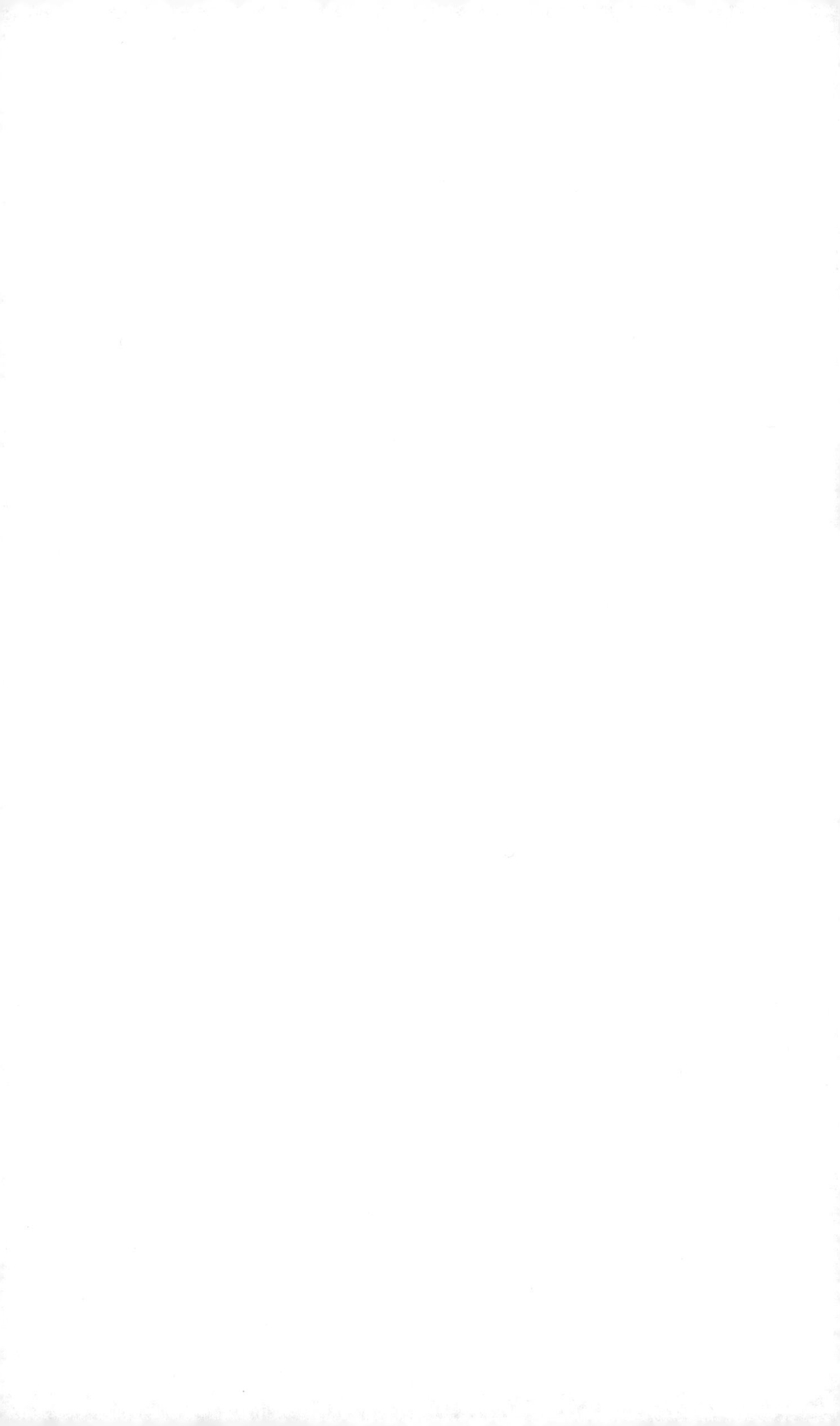

www.ingramcontent.com/pod-product-compliance
Lightning Source LLC
Chambersburg PA
CBHW051523150726
47997CB00001B/367